THE LITTLE HANDBOOK OF WINDOWS MEMORY ANALYSIS

Just some thoughts about memory, Forensics and Volatility!

Andrea Fortuna

Andrea Fortuna

This book is dedicated to all readers of my website "So Long, and Thanks for All the Fish", whose comments have contributed to the growth of website itself and my personal knowledge.

CONTENTS

Introduction 9

1. Some thoughts about Windows memory 11

  Some fundamentals 12

    The paging 12

    The TLB (Translation Lookaside Buffer) 14

  The Window Memory management 15

    Virtual Memory 16

  Memory exploitation techniques 17

    No eXecute 17

    Address Space Layout Randomization 19

2. The Volatility Framework 21

  2.1   Image Identification 23

    2.1.1   imageinfo 24

    2.1.2   kdbgscan 26

    2.1.3   Kpcrscan 28

  2.2   Kernel Memory and Objects 31

    2.2.1   modules 31

    2.2.2   modscan 33

    2.2.3   moddump 34

    2.2.4   ssdt 35

    2.2.5   driverscan 37

    2.2.6   filescan 38

    2.2.7   mutantscan 39

    2.2.8   symlinkscan 40

    2.2.9   thrdscan 41

2.2.10   dumpfiles.. 42

2.2.11   unloadedmodules... 45

2.3   Processes and DLLs.. 47

2.3.1   pslist.. 47

2.3.2   pstree.. 49

2.3.3   psscan... 50

2.3.4   psdispscan 51

2.3.5   dlllist and ldrmodules... 52

2.3.6   dlldump... 54

2.3.7   Handles... 56

2.3.8   getsids.. 58

2.3.9   cmdscan... 59

2.3.10   consoles 61

2.3.11   privs.. 64

2.3.12   envars 65

2.3.13   verinfo 66

2.3.14   enumfunc.. 67

2.4   Process Memory.. 69

2.4.1   memmap 69

2.4.2   memdump... 70

2.4.3   procdump 71

2.4.4   vadinfo... 72

2.4.5   vadwalk.. 73

2.4.6   vadtree 73

2.4.7   vaddump... 75

2.4.8   evtlogs 77

2.4.9   iehistory... 78

2.5   Networking 79

2.5.1   connections 79

2.5.2   connscan 80

2.5.3   sockets 81

2.5.4   sockscan 82

2.5.5   netscan 83

2.6   Filesystem 85

2.6.1   mbrparser 85

2.6.2   mftparser 88

2.7   Windows Registry 93

2.7.1   Hivescan 93

2.7.2   hivelist 94

2.7.3   printkey 95

2.7.4   hivedump 98

2.7.5   hashdump 99

2.7.6   lsadump 101

2.7.7   userassist 103

2.7.8   shellbags 104

2.7.9   shimcache 107

2.7.10   getservicesids 108

2.7.11   dumpregistry 109

2.8   Analyze and convert crash dumps and hibernation files 113

2.8.1   crashinfo 114

2.8.2   hibinfo 115

2.8.3   imagecopy 116

2.8.4   raw2dmp 117

2.8.5   vboxinfo 117

2.8.6   vmwareinfo... 118

2.8.7   hpakinfo.. 119

2.8.8   hpakextract... 119

3.   Memory Analysis Workflows....................................... 121

3.1   Memory acquisition on physical system 122

3.1.1   DumpIt.. 123

3.1.2   FTK Imager 125

3.1.3   WinPmem 129

3.2   Memory acquisition from a Virtual Machine 133

3.2.1   Virtual Box 133

3.2.2   VMware 136

3.3   Memory extraction from hibernation files............ 137

3.4   Extract forensic artifacts from pagefile.sys 139

3.5   Find malware in memory dumps............................ 143

3.6   Timeline creation.. 149

Required tools 149

The process.. 149

INTRODUCTION

On my previous *DIFIR related* book, "**The Little Handbook of Windows Forensic**", I addressed with an high level approach a lot of topics about forensics acquisition and analysis on windows system.

As a result of this kind of approach, the chapter about memory analysis was very small: a major shortcoming, considering the high number of forensic artifacts which can be extracted from this source.

So, this handbook is dedicated to a deep dive on Microsoft Windows memory, starting from a brief description of memory management, moving on to an extended reference of Volatility Framework and coming to a list of acquisition and analysis workflows.

Please note

As in the previous book, this manual is designed for experienced readers: in many cases I naturally assumed that some technical concepts have already fully known by readers.

For this reason, my email address is available for any clarification: you can find my public contacts on my persona website https://www.andreafortuna.org.

I'll answer everybody: slowly, but everybody, I promise!

1. SOME THOUGHTS ABOUT WINDOWS MEMORY

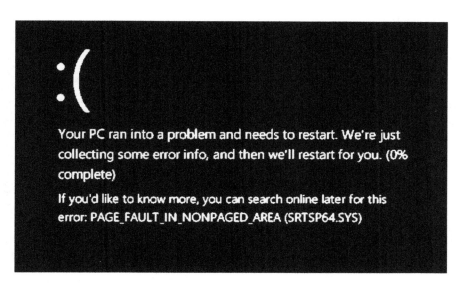

SOME FUNDAMENTALS

Just some basic information, necessary to understand the remainder of this book.

The paging

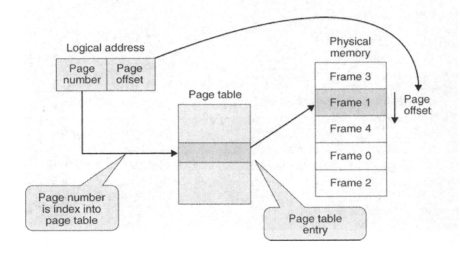

Paging is a memory management scheme by which a computer stores and retrieves data from secondary storage for use in main memory, used for to realize virtual address spaces and abstract from their physical memory.

The virtual memory is divided into equal sized pages and the physical memory into frames of the same size, and each page can be mapped to a frame.

Pages that are currently not mapped are temporarily stored on secondary storage (e.g. in a pagefile on the hard disk): when needed, the os retrieves the frame mapped to the physical page from the secondary storage.

The mapping between virtual and physical addresses normally is done transparently to the running applications by the memory management unit (MMU), which is a dedicated part of the CPU.

Under particular conditions, the hardware cannot be able to resolve the mapping without the help of the OS: in this case, a page fault error is raised and it will handled by the page fault handler of the OS.

For managing the paging mechanism, the Memory Management Unit use specific data structures, the page tables: address spaces of different processes are isolated from each other so each process uses its own instances of these structures.

Each page table entry (PTE) describes the memory range of one associated page and in order to locate the PTE which is associated to a particular memory address, it is split into two parts: the upper bits are an index into the page table, and the lower bits are used as offset to the start address of the relating frame.

The TLB (Translation Lookaside Buffer)

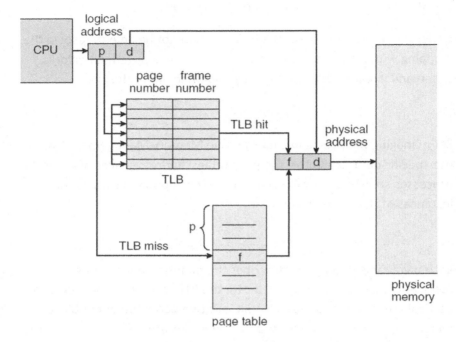

A translation lookaside buffer is a memory cache used to reduce the time necessary to access a memory location.

Part of the MMU, the TLB stores the recent translations from virtual memory to physical memory and may reside between the CPU and the CPU cache, between CPU cache and the main memory or between the different levels of the multi-level cache.

Sometimes there are distinct TLBs for data and instruction addresses, the x86 architecture offers a DTLB for the former and an ITLB for the latter one.

Normally the **DTLB** and **ITLB** are synchronized, but there are cases in which they are enforced to become unsynchronized, for example to start packed applications or to realize memory cloaking, a technique which use memory dependence prediction to speculatively identify dependent loads and stores it early in the pipeline.

THE WINDOW MEMORY MANAGEMENT

Windows has both physical and virtual memory. Memory is managed in pages, with processes demanding it as necessary. Memory pages are 4KB in size (both for physical and virtual memory).

On **32-bit (x86)** architectures, the total addressable memory is **4GB**, divided equally into user space and system space.

Pages in system space can only be accessed from kernel mode; user-mode processes (application code) can only access data that is appropriately marked in user mode.

There is one single **2GB** system space that is mapped into the address space for all processes; each process also has its own **2GB** user space.

With a **64-bit** architecture, the total address space is theoretically **16 Exabyte** (10^{18} bytes, 1 million terabytes), but for a variety of software and hardware architectural reasons, 64-bit Windows only supports **16TB** today, split equally between user and system space.

Virtual Memory

Within a process, virtual memory is broken into three categories:

- **private virtual memory**: that which is not shared, such as the process heap

- **shareable**: memory mapped files

- **free**: memory with an as yet undefined use.

Private and shareable memory can also be flagged in two ways: **reserved** (a thread has plans to use this range but it isn't available yet), and **committed** (available to use).

MEMORY EXPLOITATION TECHNIQUES

So, now let's look the most known memory protection technique, and how attackers can try to avoid them.

No eXecute

The most used technique is called **No eXecute (NX)**, first introduced under with **OpenBSD** 3.3 in May 2003.

The aim of this technique is to enforce the distinction between data and code memory: initially there was no differentiation between code and data, so each byte in memory can either be used as code, if its address is loaded into the instruction pointer, or it can be used as data if it is accessed by a load or store operation.

An unwanted side effect of this is that attackers are able to conceal malicious code as harmless data and then later on, with the help of some vulnerability, execute it as code.

The **NX** protection is implemented by hardware on contemporary **CPU** but can be also simulated in software (usually named **DEP – Data Execution Prevention** on Windows systems).

On newer **x86/x64** machines there is one dedicated **PTE** flag that controls if a certain page is executable or not.

If this flag is set, a page fault is invoked on the attempt to execute code from the corresponding page.

Therefore, besides the hardware, also the operating system has to implement this security feature as well.

In order to overcome the **NX** protection, attackers use different methods.

One very powerful way is to locate and execute useful instructions in one of the loaded system or application library modules: for example, in Return Oriented Programming (**ROP**) attackers do not call complete library functions, but instead they use only small code chunks are already present in the machine's memory and chain those together to implement their desired functionality.

This instruction sequences are called "**gadgets**".

Each gadget typically ends in a return instruction and is located in a subroutine within the existing program and/or shared library code.

Chained together, these gadgets allow an attacker to perform arbitrary operations on a machine.

Address Space Layout Randomization

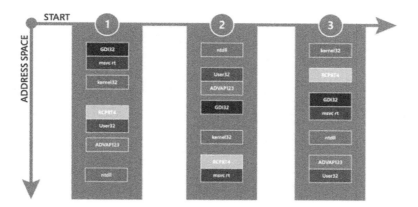

Address Space Layout Randomization (**ASLR**) is mechanism that makes all memory locations no longer fixed and predictable, but chosen randomly.

Consequently, the stack, the heap and the loaded modules will have different memory addresses each time a process is started making much harder for attackers to find usable memory locations, such as the beginning of a certain function or the effective location of malicious code or data.

Accordingly, when the memory layout is randomized and an exploit is performed that does not take this into account, the process will rather crash than being exploited.

One possible attack approach is to locate and utilize non-randomized memory, since early implementations of **ASLR** do not randomize the complete memory but only some parts of it.

Furthermore, Windows allows the disabling of **ASLR** on a per-module-base: so, even if all Windows libraries are ASLR-protected, a lot of custom libraries are not and constitute an easy exploitation target for attackers.

For example, in the old **CVE-2010-3971** the protection could be bypassed using the IE DLL mscorie.dll, that was distributed with ASLR disabled.

2. THE VOLATILITY FRAMEWORK

THE FRAMEWORK

The Volatility Framework is a completely open collection of tools, implemented in Python under the GNU General Public License (GPL v2), for the extraction of digital artifacts from volatile memory samples.

It is the world's most widely used memory forensics platform for digital investigations.

It supports memory dumps from all major 32- and 64-bit Windows, Linux and Mac operating systems, and the extraction techniques are performed completely independent of the system being investigated but offer unprecedented visibility into the runtime state of the system.

The Volatility Framework was designed to be expanded by plugins: here a brief reference of most used plugins.

2.1   IMAGE IDENTIFICATION

In order to start a memory analysis with Volatility, the identification of the type of memory image is a mandatory step.

2.1.1   imageinfo

For a high level summary of the memory sample you're analyzing, use
the **imageinfo** command.

Most often this command is used to identify the operating system,
service pack, and hardware architecture (32 or 64 bit), but it also
contains other useful information such as the **DTB** address and time the
sample was collected.

```
$ vol.py -f win7.raw imageinfo

Volatility Foundation Volatility Framework 2.6
Determining profile based on KDBG search...

Suggested Profile(s) : Win7SP0x64, Win7SP1x64, Win2008R2SP0x64, Win2008R2SP1x64
                AS Layer1 : AMD64PagedMemory (Kernel AS)
                AS Layer2 : FileAddressSpace (/Users/Michael/Desktop/win7.raw)
                PAE type : PAE
                    DTB : 0x187000L
                   KDBG : 0xf80002803070
        Number of Processors : 1
     Image Type (Service Pack) : 0
           KPCR for CPU 0 : 0xfffff80002804d00L
          KUSER_SHARED_DATA : 0xfffff78000000000L
          Image date and time : 2012-02-22 11:29:02 UTC+0000
        Image local date and time : 2012-02-22 03:29:02 -0800
```

The **imageinfo** output tells you the suggested profile that you should
pass as the parameter to --profile=PROFILE when using other plugins.
There may be more than one profile suggestion if profiles are closely
related. It also prints the address of the KDBG (short
for _KDDEBUGGER_DATA64) structure that will be used by plugins like
pslist and modules to find the process and module list heads,
respectively.

In some cases, especially larger memory samples, there may be multiple
KDBG structures. Similarly, if there are multiple processors, you'll see
the KPCR address and CPU number for each one.

Plugins automatically scan for the KPCR and KDBG values when they need them. However, you can specify the values directly for any plugin by providing **--kpcr=ADDRESS** or **--kdbg=ADDRESS**.

By supplying the profile and KDBG (or failing that KPCR) to other Volatility commands, you'll get the most accurate and fastest results possible.

Note: The **imageinfo** plugin will not work on hibernation files unless the correct profile is given in advance. This is because important structure definitions vary between different operating systems.

The KDBG is a structure maintained by the Windows kernel for debugging purposes. It contains a list of the running processes and loaded kernel modules. It also contains some information that allows you to determine from which Windows version came the memory dump, what Service Pack was installed, and the memory model (32-bit vs 64-bit).

2.1.2 kdbgscan

As opposed to **imageinfo** which simply provides profile suggestions, **kdbgscan** is designed to positively identify the correct profile and the correct KDBG address (if there happen to be multiple).

This plugin scans for the **KDBGHeader** signatures linked to Volatility profiles and applies sanity checks to reduce false positives. The verbosity of the output and number of sanity checks that can be performed depends on whether Volatility can find a **DTB**, so if you already know the correct profile (or if you have a profile suggestion from **imageinfo**), then make sure you use it.

Here's an example scenario of when this plugin can be useful. You have a memory sample that you believe to be **Windows 2003 SP2 x64**, but **pslist** doesn't show any processes.

The **pslist** plugin relies on finding the process list head which is pointed to by KDBG. However, the plugin takes the *first* KDBG found in the memory sample, which is not always the *best* one.

You may run into this problem if a KDBG with an invalid PsActiveProcessHead pointer is found earlier in a sample (i.e. at a lower physical offset) than the valid KDBG.

Notice below how kdbgscan picks up two KDBG structures: an invalid one (with 0 processes and 0 modules) is found first at 0xf80001172cb0 and a valid one (with 37 processes and 116 modules) is found next at 0xf80001175cf0.

In order to "fix" pslist for this sample, you would simply need to supply the **--kdbg=0xf80001175cf0** to the **plist** plugin.

```
$ vol.py -f Win2K3SP2x64-6f1bedec.vmem --profile=Win2003SP2x64 kdbgscan

Volatility Foundation Volatility Framework 2.6
**************************************************
Instantiating KDBG using: Kernel AS Win2003SP2x64 (5.2.3791 64bit)
Offset (V)              : 0xf80001172cb0
Offset (P)              : 0x1172cb0
KDBG owner tag check        : True
Profile suggestion (KDBGHeader): Win2003SP2x64
Version64               : 0xf80001172c70 (Major: 15, Minor: 3790)
Service Pack (CmNtCSDVersion) : 0
Build string (NtBuildLab)   : T?
PsActiveProcessHead         : 0xfffff800011947f0 (0 processes)
PsLoadedModuleList          : 0xfffff80001197ac0 (0 modules)
KernelBase              : 0xfffff80001000000 (Matches MZ: True)
Major (OptionalHeader)      : 5
Minor (OptionalHeader)      : 2

**************************************************
Instantiating KDBG using: Kernel AS Win2003SP2x64 (5.2.3791 64bit)
Offset (V)              : 0xf80001175cf0
Offset (P)              : 0x1175cf0
KDBG owner tag check        : True
Profile suggestion (KDBGHeader): Win2003SP2x64
Version64               : 0xf80001175cb0 (Major: 15, Minor: 3790)
Service Pack (CmNtCSDVersion) : 2
Build string (NtBuildLab)   : 3790.srv03_sp2_rtm.070216-1710
PsActiveProcessHead         : 0xfffff800011977f0 (37 processes)
PsLoadedModuleList          : 0xfffff8000119aae0 (116 modules)
KernelBase              : 0xfffff80001000000 (Matches MZ: True)
Major (OptionalHeader)      : 5
Minor (OptionalHeader)      : 2
KPCR                    : 0xfffff80001177000 (CPU 0)
```

2.1.3 Kpcrscan

Use this command to scan for potential **KPCR** structures by checking for the self-referencing members as described by Finding Object Roots in Vista.

*The KPCR stands for **K**ernel **P**rocessor **C**ontrol **R**egion. Is a data structure used by the Windows kernel to store information about each processor.*

On a multi-core system, each processor has its own KPCR. Therefore, you'll see details for each processor, including IDT and GDT address; current, idle, and next threads; CPU number, vendor & speed; and CR3 value.

```
$ vol.py -f dang_win7_x64.raw --profile=Win7SP1x64 kpcrscan

Volatility Foundation Volatility Framework 2.6
**************************************************
Offset (V)            : 0xf800029ead00
Offset (P)            : 0x29ead00
KdVersionBlock         : 0x0
IDT                  : 0xfffff80000b95080
GDT                  : 0xfffff80000b95000
CurrentThread          : 0xfffffa800cf694d0 TID 2148 (kd.exe:2964)
IdleThread             : 0xfffff800029f8c40 TID 0 (Idle:0)
Details              : CPU 0 (GenuineIntel @ 2128 MHz)
CR3/DTB               : 0x1dcec000
**************************************************
Offset (V)            : 0xf880009e7000
Offset (P)            : 0x4d9e000
KdVersionBlock         : 0x0
IDT                  : 0xfffff880009f2540
GDT                  : 0xfffff880009f24c0
CurrentThread          : 0xfffffa800cf694d0 TID 2148 (kd.exe:2964)
IdleThread             : 0xfffff880009f1f40 TID 0 (Idle:0)
Details              : CPU 1 (GenuineIntel @ 2220 MHz)
CR3/DTB               : 0x1dcec000
```

If the **KdVersionBlock** is not null, then it may be possible to find the machine's KDBG address via the **KPCR**.

In fact, the backup method of finding KDBG used by plugins such as pslist is to leverage kpcrscan and then call the KPCR.get_kdbg() API function.

2.2 KERNEL MEMORY AND OBJECTS

2.2.1 modules

To view the list of kernel drivers loaded on the system, use the modules command. This walks the doubly-linked list of **LDR_DATA_TABLE_ENTRY**structures pointed to by **PsLoadedModuleList**.

Similar to the pslist command, this relies on finding the KDBG structure. In rare cases, you may need to use kdbgscan to find the most appropriate KDBG structure address and then supply it to this plugin like **--kdbg=ADDRESS**.

It cannot find hidden/unlinked kernel drivers, however **modscan** serves that purpose.

Also, since this plugin uses list walking techniques, you typically can assume that the order the modules are displayed in the output is the order they were loaded on the system. For example, below, **ntoskrnl.exe** was first to load, followed by hal.dll, etc.

```
$ vol.py -f win7.raw --profile=Win7SP0x64 modules

Volatility Foundation Volatility Framework 2.6
Offset(V)          Name                  Base                    Size File
------------------ --------------------- ------------------ ------------------ ----
0xffffffa80004a11a0 ntoskrnl.exe         0xfffff8000261a000       0x5dd000
\SystemRoot\system32\ntoskrnl.exe
0xffffffa80004a10b0 hal.dll              0xfffff80002bf7000       0x49000 \SystemRoot\system32\hal.dll
0xffffffa80004a7950 kdcom.dll            0xfffff80000bb4000       0xa000
\SystemRoot\system32\kdcom.dll
0xffffffa80004a7860 mcupdate.dll         0xfffff88000c3a000       0x44000
\SystemRoot\system32\mcupdate_GenuineIntel.dll
0xffffffa80004a7780 PSHED.dll            0xfffff88000c7e000       0x14000
\SystemRoot\system32\PSHED.dll
0xffffffa80004a7690 CLFS.SYS             0xfffff88000c92000       0x5e000
\SystemRoot\system32\CLFS.SYS
0xffffffa80004a8010 CI.dll               0xfffff88000cf0000       0xc0000 \SystemRoot\system32\CI.dll
...
```

The output shows the offset of the **LDR_DATA_TABLE_ENTRY** structure, which is a virtual address by default but can be specified as a physical address with the -P switch as shown below. In either case, the Base column is the virtual address of the module's base in kernel memory (where you'd expect to find the PE header).

```
$ vol.py -f win7.raw --profile=Win7SP0x64 modules -P

Volatility Foundation Volatility Framework 2.6
Offset(P)          Name              Base                 Size File
------------------ ----------------- ------------------ ------------------- ----
0x0000000017fe01a0 ntoskrnl.exe      0xfffff8000261a000      0x5dd000
\SystemRoot\system32\ntoskrnl.exe
0x0000000017fe00b0 hal.dll           0xfffff80002bf7000      0x49000 \SystemRoot\system32\hal.dll
0x0000000017fe6950 kdcom.dll         0xfffff80000bb4000      0xa000
\SystemRoot\system32\kdcom.dll
0x0000000017fe6860 mcupdate.dll      0xfffff88000c3a000      0x44000
\SystemRoot\system32\mcupdate_GenuineIntel.dll
0x0000000017fe6780 PSHED.dll         0xfffff88000c7e000      0x14000
\SystemRoot\system32\PSHED.dll
0x0000000017fe6690 CLFS.SYS          0xfffff88000c92000      0x5e000
\SystemRoot\system32\CLFS.SYS
0x0000000017fe7010 CI.dll            0xfffff88000cf0000      0xc0000 \SystemRoot\system32\CI.dll
...
```

2.2.2   modscan

The **modscan** command finds **LDR_DATA_TABLE_ENTRY** structures by scanning physical memory for pool tags.

This can pick up previously unloaded drivers and drivers that have been hidden/unlinked by rootkits. Unlike modules the order of results has no relationship with the order in which the drivers loaded. As you can see below, DumpIt.sys was found at the lowest physical offset, but it was probably one of the last drivers to load (since it was used to acquire memory).

```
$ vol.py -f win7.raw --profile=Win7SP0x64 modscan

Volatility Foundation Volatility Framework 2.6
Offset(P)        Name           Base               Size File
---------------- -------------------- ------------------ ------------------- ----
0x00000000173b90b0 DumpIt.sys       0xfffff88003980000      0x11000
\??\C:\Windows\SysWOW64\Drivers\DumpIt.sys
0x000000001745b180 mouhid.sys       0xfffff880037e9000      0xd000
\SystemRoot\system32\DRIVERS\mouhid.sys
0x0000000017473010 lltdio.sys       0xfffff88002585000      0x15000
\SystemRoot\system32\DRIVERS\lltdio.sys
0x000000001747f010 rspndr.sys       0xfffff8800259a000      0x18000
\SystemRoot\system32\DRIVERS\rspndr.sys
0x00000000174cac40 dxg.sys          0xfffff96000440000      0x1e000
\SystemRoot\System32\drivers\dxg.sys
0x0000000017600190 monitor.sys      0xfffff8800360c000      0xe000
\SystemRoot\system32\DRIVERS\monitor.sys
0x0000000017601170 HIDPARSE.SYS     0xfffff880037de000      0x9000
\SystemRoot\system32\DRIVERS\HIDPARSE.SYS
0x0000000017604180 USBD.SYS         0xfffff880037e7000      0x2000
\SystemRoot\system32\DRIVERS\USBD.SYS
0x0000000017611d70 cdrom.sys        0xfffff88001944000      0x2a000
\SystemRoot\system32\DRIVERS\cdrom.sys
...
```

2.2.3   moddump

To extract a kernel driver to a file, use the **moddump** command.
Supply the output directory with **-D** or **--dump-dir=DIR**.
Without any additional parameters, all drivers identified by modlist will
be dumped. If you want a specific driver, supply a regular expression of
the driver's name with **--regex=REGEX** or the module's base address
with **--base=BASE**.

```
$ vol.py -f win7.raw --profile=Win7SP0x64 moddump -D drivers/

Volatility Foundation Volatility Framework 2.6
Module Base       Module Name        Result
----------------- ------------------ ------
0xfffff8000261a000 ntoskrnl.exe       OK: driver.fffff8000261a000.sys
0xfffff80002bf7000 hal.dll            OK: driver.fffff80002bf7000.sys
0xfffff88000e5c000 intelide.sys       OK: driver.fffff88000e5c000.sys
0xfffff8800349b000 mouclass.sys       OK: driver.fffff8800349b000.sys
0xfffff88000f7c000 msisadrv.sys       OK: driver.fffff88000f7c000.sys
0xfffff880035c3000 ndistapi.sys       OK: driver.fffff880035c3000.sys
0xfffff88002c5d000 pacer.sys          OK: driver.fffff88002c5d000.sys
...
```

Similar to **dlldump**, if critical parts of the PE header are not memory
resident, then rebuilding/extracting the driver may fail.

Additionally, for drivers that are mapped in different sessions (like
win32k.sys), there is currently no way to specify which session to use
when acquiring the driver sample.

2.2.4   ssdt

To list the functions in the Native and GUI System Service Dispatch Table (SSDT), use the ssdt command.

This displays the index, function name, and owning driver for each entry in the SSDT. Please note the following:

- **Windows** has 4 SSDTs by default (you can add more with **KeAddSystemServiceTable**), but only 2 of them are used — one for Native functions in the NT module, and one for GUI functions in the win32k.sys module.
- There are multiple ways to locate the SSDTs in memory. Most tools do it by finding the exported **KeServiceDescriptorTable** symbol in the NT module, but this is not the way Volatility works.
- For **x86** systems, Volatility scans for ETHREAD objects and gathers all unique ETHREAD.Tcb.ServiceTable pointers.
  This method is more robust and complete, because it can detect when rootkits make copies of the existing SSDTs and assign them to particular threads.
  Also see the threads command.
- For **x64** systems (which do not have an ETHREAD.Tcb.ServiceTable member) Volatility disassembles code in **ntKeAddSystemServiceTable** and finds its references to the **KeServiceDescriptorTable** and **KeServiceDescriptorTableShadow** symbols.
- The order and total number of functions in the SSDTs differ across operating system versions. Thus, Volatility stores the information in a per-profile (OS) dictionary which is auto-generated and cross-referenced using the ntoskrnl.exe, ntdll.dll, win32k.sys, user32.dll and gdi32.dll modules from the respective systems.

```
$ vol.py -f win7.raw --profile=Win7SP0x64 ssdt

Volatility Foundation Volatility Framework 2.6
[x64] Gathering all referenced SSDTs from KeAddSystemServiceTable...
Finding appropriate address space for tables...
SSDT[0] at fffff8000268cb00 with 401 entries
  Entry 0x0000: 0xfffff80002a9d190 (NtMapUserPhysicalPagesScatter) owned by
ntoskrnl.exe
  Entry 0x0001: 0xfffff80002983a00 (NtWaitForSingleObject) owned by ntoskrnl.exe
  Entry 0x0002: 0xfffff80002683dd0 (NtCallbackReturn) owned by ntoskrnl.exe
  Entry 0x0003: 0xfffff800029a6b10 (NtReadFile) owned by ntoskrnl.exe
  Entry 0x0004: 0xfffff800029a4bb0 (NtDeviceIoControlFile) owned by ntoskrnl.exe
  Entry 0x0005: 0xfffff8000299fee0 (NtWriteFile) owned by ntoskrnl.exe
  Entry 0x0006: 0xfffff80002945dc0 (NtRemoveIoCompletion) owned by ntoskrnl.exe
  Entry 0x0007: 0xfffff80002942f10 (NtReleaseSemaphore) owned by ntoskrnl.exe
  Entry 0x0008: 0xfffff8000299ada0 (NtReplyWaitReceivePort) owned by ntoskrnl.exe
  Entry 0x0009: 0xfffff80002a6ce20 (NtReplyPort) owned by ntoskrnl.exe
[...]
SSDT[1] at fffff96000101c00 with 827 entries
  Entry 0x1000: 0xfffff960000f5580 (NtUserGetThreadState) owned by win32k.sys
  Entry 0x1001: 0xfffff960000f2630 (NtUserPeekMessage) owned by win32k.sys
  Entry 0x1002: 0xfffff96000103c6c (NtUserCallOneParam) owned by win32k.sys
  Entry 0x1003: 0xfffff96000111dd0 (NtUserGetKeyState) owned by win32k.sys
  Entry 0x1004: 0xfffff9600010b1ac (NtUserInvalidateRect) owned by win32k.sys
  Entry 0x1005: 0xfffff96000103e70 (NtUserCallNoParam) owned by win32k.sys
  Entry 0x1006: 0xfffff960000fb5a0 (NtUserGetMessage) owned by win32k.sys
  Entry 0x1007: 0xfffff960000dfbec (NtUserMessageCall) owned by win32k.sys
  Entry 0x1008: 0xfffff96000101056c4 (NtGdiBitBlt) owned by win32k.sys
  Entry 0x1009: 0xfffff960001fd750 (NtGdiGetCharSet) owned by win32k.sys
```

To filter all functions which point to ntoskrnl.exe and win32k.sys, you can use egrep on command-line. This will only show hooked SSDT functions.

```
$ vol.py -f win7.raw --profile=Win7SP0x64 ssdt | egrep -v '(ntos|win32k)'
```

Note that the NT module on your system may be ntkrnlpa.exe or ntkrnlmp.exe — so check that before using egrep of you'll be filtering the wrong module name.

Also be aware that this isn't a hardened technique for finding hooks, as malware can load a driver named **win32ktesting.sys** and bypass your filter.

2.2.5   driverscan

To find **DRIVER_OBJECT**s in physical memory using pool tag scanning, use the driverscan command.

This is another way to locate kernel modules, although not all kernel modules have an associated **DRIVER_OBJECT**.

The **DRIVER_OBJECT** is what contains the 28 IRP (Major Function) tables, thus the driverirp command is based on the methodology used by driverscan.

```
$ vol.py -f win7.raw --profile=Win7SP0x64 driverscan

Volatility Foundation Volatility Framework 2.6
Offset(P)        #Ptr #Hnd Start                      Size Service Key        Name       Driver Name
------------------ ---- ---- --------------------- -------------------- -------------------- ------------ -----------
0x00000000174c6350  3    0 0xfffff880037e9000        0xd000 mouhid           mouhid     \Driver\mouhid
0x000000017660cb0   3    0 0xfffff8800259a000        0x18000 rspndr          rspndr     \Driver\rspndr
0x0000000017663e70  3    0 0xfffff88002585000        0x15000 lltdio          lltdio     \Driver\lltdio
0x0000000017691d70  3    0 0xfffff88001944000        0x2a000 cdrom           cdrom      \Driver\cdrom
0x0000000017692a50  3    0 0xfffff8800196e000        0x9000 Null            Null       \Driver\Null
0x0000000017695e70  3    0 0xfffff88001977000        0x7000 Beep            Beep       \Driver\Beep
0x00000000176965c0  3    0 0xfffff8800197e000        0xe000 VgaSave         VgaSave    \Driver\VgaSave
0x000000001769fb00  4    0 0xfffff880019c1000        0x9000 RDPCDD          RDPCDD     \Driver\RDPCDD
0x00000000176a1720  3    0 0xfffff880019ca000        0x9000 RDPENCDD        RDPENCDD   \Driver\RDPENCDD
0x00000000176a2230  3    0 0xfffff880019d3000        0x9000 RDPREFMP        RDPREFMP   \Driver\RDPREFMP
...
```

2.2.6 filescan

To find **FILE_OBJECT**s in physical memory using pool tag scanning, use the filescan command. This will find open files even if a rootkit is hiding the files on disk and if the rootkit hooks some API functions to hide the open handles on a live system. The output shows the physical offset of the **FILE_OBJECT**, file name, number of pointers to the object, number of handles to the object, and the effective permissions granted to the object.

```
$ vol.py -f win7.raw --profile=Win7SP0x64 filescan

Volatility Foundation Volatility Framework 2.6
Offset(P)            #Ptr   #Hnd Access Name
------------------ ------ ------ ------ ----
0x000000000126f3a0    14      0 R--r-d \Windows\System32\mswsock.dll
0x000000000126fdc0    11      0 R--r-d \Windows\System32\ssdpsrv.dll
0x000000000468f7e0     6      0 R--r-d \Windows\System32\cryptsp.dll
0x000000000468fdc0    16      0 R--r-d \Windows\System32\Apphlpdm.dll
0x00000000048223a0     1      1 ------ \Endpoint
0x0000000004822a30    16      0 R--r-d \Windows\System32\kerberos.dll
0x0000000004906070    13      0 R--r-d \Windows\System32\wbem\repdrvfs.dll
0x0000000004906580     9      0 R--r-d \Windows\SysWOW64\netprofm.dll
0x0000000004906bf0     9      0 R--r-d \Windows\System32\wbem\wmiutils.dll
0x00000000049ce8e0     2      1 R--rwd \$Extend\$ObjId
0x00000000049cedd0     1      1 R--r-d \Windows\System32\en-US\vsstrace.dll.mui
0x0000000004a71070    17      1 R--r-d \Windows\System32\en-US\pnidui.dll.mui
0x0000000004a71440    11      0 R--r-d \Windows\System32\nci.dll
0x0000000004a719c0     1      1 ------ \srvsvc
...
```

2.2.7   mutantscan

To scan physical memory for **KMUTANT** objects with pool tag scanning, use the **mutantscan** command.

By default, it displays all objects, but you can pass -s or — silent to only show named **mutexes**.

The CID column contains the process ID and thread ID of the **mutex** owner if one exists.

```
$ vol.py -f win7.raw --profile=Win7SP0x64 mutantscan –silent

Volatility Foundation Volatility Framework 2.6

Offset(P)        #Ptr #Hnd Signal Thread            CID Name
------------------ ---- ---- ------ ------------------ --------- ----
0x000000000f702630  2    1     1 0x0000000000000000           {A3BD3259-3E4F-428a-84C8-
F0463A9D3EB5}
0x0000000102fd930   2    1     1 0x0000000000000000           Feed Arbitration Shared Memory Mutex
[ User : S-1-5-21-2628989162-3383567662-1028919141-1000 ]
0x00000000104e5e60  3    2     1 0x0000000000000000           ZoneAttributeCacheCounterMutex
0x000000010c29e40   2    1     1 0x0000000000000000           _MSFTHISTORY_LOW_
0x0000000013035080  2    1     1 0x0000000000000000
c:userstestingappdatalocalmicrosoftfeeds cache
0x000000001722dfc0  2    1     1 0x0000000000000000
c:userstestingappdataroamingmicrosoftwindowsietldcachelow
0x00000000172497f0  2    1     1 0x0000000000000000           LRIEElevationPolicyMutex
0x000000001724bfc0  3    2     1 0x0000000000000000           BrowserEmulationSharedMemoryMutex
0x000000001724f400  2    1     1 0x0000000000000000
c:userstestingappdatalocalmicrosoftwindowshistorylowhistory.ie5mshist012012022220120223
0x000000001724f4c0  4    3     1 0x0000000000000000           _SHMSFTHISTORY_
0x00000000172517c0  2    1     1 0x0000000000000000           __DDrawExclMode__
0x00000000172783a0  2    1     1 0x0000000000000000           Lowhttp://sourceforge.net/
0x00000000172db840  4    3     1 0x0000000000000000
ConnHashTable<1892>_HashTable_Mutex
0x00000000172de1d0  2    1     1 0x0000000000000000           Feeds Store Mutex S-1-5-21-
2628989162-3383567662-1028919141-1000
0x00000000173b8080  2    1     1 0x0000000000000000           DDrawDriverObjectListMutex
0x00000000173bd340  2    1     0 0xfffffa8000a216d0 1652:2000 ALTTAB_RUNNING_MUTEX
0x0000000017449c40  2    1     1 0x0000000000000000           DDrawWindowListMutex
...
```

2.2.8   symlinkscan

This plugin scans for symbolic link objects and outputs their information.
In the past, this has been used to link drive letters (i.e. D:, E:, F:, etc) to true crypt volumes (i.e. \Device\TrueCryptVolume).

$ vol.py -f win7.raw --profile=Win7SP0x64 symlinkscan

```
Volatility Foundation Volatility Framework 2.6
Offset(P)          #Ptr  #Hnd Creation time          From              To
------------------ ------ ------ --------------------- ------------------- -----------------------------------------
-------------------
0x0000000000469780   1    0 2012-02-22 20:03:13    UMB#UMB#1...e1ba19f} \Device\00000048
0x0000000000754560   1    0 2012-02-22 20:03:15    ASYNCMAC          \Device\ASYNCMAC
0x00000000000ef6cf0   2    1 2012-02-22 19:58:24    0                \BaseNamedObjects
0x00000000014b2a10   1    0 2012-02-22 20:02:10    LanmanRedirector
\Device\Mup\;LanmanRedirector
0x00000000053e56f0   1    0 2012-02-22 20:03:15    SW#{eeab7...abac361}
\Device\KSENUM#00000001
0x0000000005cc0770   1    0 2012-02-22 19:58:20    WanArpV6          \Device\WANARPV6
0x0000000005cc0820   1    0 2012-02-22 19:58:20    WanArp           \Device\WANARP
0x0000000008ffa680   1    0 2012-02-22 19:58:24    Global           \BaseNamedObjects
0x0000000009594810   1    0 2012-02-22 19:58:24    KnownDllPath      C:\Windows\syswow64
0x000000000968f5f0   1    0 2012-02-22 19:58:23    KnownDllPath      C:\Windows\system32
0x000000000ab24060   1    0 2012-02-22 19:58:20    Volume{3b...f6e6963} \Device\CdRom0
0x000000000ab24220   1    0 2012-02-22 19:58:21    {EE0434CC...863ACC2} \Device\NDMP2
0x000000000abd3460   1    0 2012-02-22 19:58:21    ACPI#PNP0...91405dd} \Device\00000041
0x000000000abd36f0   1    0 2012-02-22 19:58:21    {802389A0...A90C31A} \Device\NDMP3
...
```

2.2.9 thrdscan

To find **ETHREAD** objects in physical memory with pool tag scanning, use the thrdscan command.

Since an ETHREAD contains fields that identify its parent process, you can use this technique to find hidden processes. One such use case is documented in the psxview command.

Also, for verbose details, try the threads plugin.

```
$ vol.py -f win7.raw --profile=Win7SP0x64 thrdscan

Volatility Foundation Volatility Framework 2.6
Offset(P)            PID    TID    Start Address Create Time          Exit Time
------------------- ------ ------ ------------------ ------------------------- -------------------------
0x0000000008df68d0   280    392      0x77943260 2012-02-22 19:08:18
0x000000000eac3850   2040   144      0x76d73260 2012-02-22 11:28:59   2012-02-22 11:29:04
0x000000000fd82590   880    1944     0x76d73260 2012-02-22 20:02:29   2012-02-22 20:02:29
0x00000000103d15f0   880    884      0x76d73260 2012-02-22 19:58:43
0x00000000103e5480   1652   1788 0xfffff8a0010ed490 2012-02-22 20:03:44
0x00000000105a3940   916    324      0x76d73260 2012-02-22 20:02:07   2012-02-22 20:02:09
0x00000000105b3560   816    824      0x76d73260 2012-02-22 19:58:42
0x00000000106d1710   916    1228     0x76d73260 2012-02-22 20:02:11
0x0000000010a349a0   816    820      0x76d73260 2012-02-22 19:58:41
0x0000000010bd1060   1892   2280     0x76d73260 2012-02-22 11:26:13
0x0000000010f24230   628    660      0x76d73260 2012-02-22 19:58:34
0x0000000010f27060   568    648 0xfffff8a0017c6650 2012-02-22 19:58:34
...
```

2.2.10 dumpfiles

Files are cached in memory for system performance as they are accessed and used. This makes the cache a valuable source from a forensic perspective since we are able to retrieve files that were in use correctly, instead of file carving which does not make use of how items are mapped in memory.
Files may not be completely mapped in memory (also for performance), so missing sections are zero padded. Files dumped from memory can then be processed with external tools.

There are several options in the dumpfiles plugin, for example:

```
-r REGEX, --regex=REGEX
                Dump files matching REGEX
 -i, --ignore-case    Ignore case in pattern match
 -o OFFSET, --offset=OFFSET
                Dump files for Process with physical address OFFSET
 -Q PHYSOFFSET, --physoffset=PHYSOFFSET
                Dump File Object at physical address PHYSOFFSET
 -D DUMP_DIR, --dump-dir=DUMP_DIR
                Directory in which to dump extracted files
 -S SUMMARY_FILE, --summary-file=SUMMARY_FILE
                File where to store summary information
 -p PID, --pid=PID    Operate on these Process IDs (comma-separated)
 -n, --name           Include extracted filename in output file path
 -u, --unsafe         Relax safety constraints for more data
 -F FILTER, --filter=FILTER
                Filters to apply (comma-separated)
```

By default, dumpfiles iterates through the VAD and extracts all files that are mapped as DataSectionObject, ImageSectionObject or SharedCacheMap. As an investigator, however, you may want to perform a more targeted search.

You can use the **-r** and **-i** flags to specify a case-insensitive regex of a filename. In the output below, you can see where the file was dumped from (DataSectionObject, ImageSectionObject or SharedCacheMap), the offset of the _FILE_OBJECT, the PID of the process whose VAD contained the file and the file path on disk:

```
$ vol.py -f mebromi.raw dumpfiles -D output/ -r evt$ -i -S summary.txt

Volatility Foundation Volatility Framework 2.6
DataSectionObject 0x81ed6240   684
\Device\HarddiskVolume1\WINDOWS\system32\config\AppEvent.Evt
SharedCacheMap 0x81ed6240   684
\Device\HarddiskVolume1\WINDOWS\system32\config\AppEvent.Evt
DataSectionObject 0x8217beb0   684
\Device\HarddiskVolume1\WINDOWS\system32\config\SecEvent.Evt
DataSectionObject 0x8217bd78   684
\Device\HarddiskVolume1\WINDOWS\system32\config\SysEvent.Evt
SharedCacheMap 0x8217bd78   684
\Device\HarddiskVolume1\WINDOWS\system32\config\SysEvent.Evt

$ ls output/
file.684.0x81fc6ed0.vacb    file.684.0x82256a48.dat        file.684.0x82256e48.dat
         file.None.0x82339cd8.vacb
file.684.0x8217b720.vacb    file.684.0x82256c50.dat        file.None.0x82339c70.dat
```

The dumped filename is in the format of:

```
file.[PID].[OFFSET].ext
```

The OFFSET is the offset of the SharedCacheMap or the _CONTROL_AREA, not the _FILE_OBJECT.

The extension (EXT) can be:

- img — ImageSectionObject
- dat — DataSectionObject
- vacb — SharedCacheMap

You can look at the -S/--summary-file in order to map the file back to its original filename:

```
{"name":
"\\Device\\HarddiskVolume1\\WINDOWS\\system32\\config\\AppEvent.Evt",
"ofpath": "dumpfiles/file.684.0x82256e48.dat", "pid": 684,...
```

You can also use the *parsesummary.py* script to parse out the json output of the summary file.

The following shows an example of using this script. In addition to the original file name, PID of the process that had the file open and size, you can see which pages were present and which pages were missing and padded with zeros in the parsed summary output:

```
$ vol.py -f grrcon.img dumpfiles --summary=grrcon_summary.json -D output/
Volatility Foundation Volatility Framework 2.6

$ python parsesummary.py grrcon_summary.json | less
[...]
File: \Device\HarddiskVolume1\Documents and Settings\administrator\NTUSER.DAT ->
output/file.4.0x82245008.vacb
        PID: 4
        _FILE_OBJECT offset: 0x821cd9e8
        Type: SharedCacheMap
        Size: 262144
        Present Pages:
                Offset(V): 0xde5c0000, Length: 4096
                Offset(V): 0xde5c1000, Length: 4096
                Offset(V): 0xde5c2000, Length: 4096
                Offset(V): 0xde5c3000, Length: 4096
...
        Padding:
                FileOffset: 0xde62e000 x 0x1000
                FileOffset: 0xde62f000 x 0x1000
                FileOffset: 0xde630000 x 0x1000
                FileOffset: 0xde631000 x 0x1000
                FileOffset: 0xde632000 x 0x1000
...
```

Or you can use the -n/--name option in order to dump file the files with the original filename.

Not every file will be currently active or in the VAD, and such files will not be dumped when using the -r/--regex option. For these files you can first scan for a _FILE_OBJECT and then use the -Q/--physoffset flag to extract the file. Special NTFS files are examples of files that must be dumped specifically:

```
$ vol.py -f mem.raw filescan | grep -i mft

Volatility Foundation Volatility Framework 2.6
0x02410900    3    0 RWD--- \Device\HarddiskVolume1\$Mft
0x02539e30    3    0 RWD--- \Device\HarddiskVolume1\$Mft
0x025ac868    3    0 RWD--- \Device\HarddiskVolume1\$MftMirr

$ vol.py -f mem.raw dumpfiles -D output/ -Q 0x02539e30

Volatility Foundation Volatility Framework 2.6
DataSectionObject 0x02539e30   None
\Device\HarddiskVolume1\$Mft
SharedCacheMap 0x02539e30   None   \Device\HarddiskVolume1\$Mft
```

The -f/--filter option allows you to specify which view of the file you would like to dump (DataSectionObject, ImageSectionObject or SharedCacheMap).

For example, if you wanted to only see the state information for an executable file, you could specify --filter=ImageSectionObject.

2.2.11 unloadedmodules

Windows stores information on recently unloaded drivers for debugging purposes. This gives you an alternative way to determine what happened on a system, besides the well-known modules and modscan plugins.

```
$ vol.py -f win7.raw unloadedmodules --profile=Win7SP0x64

Volatility Foundation Volatility Framework 2.6
Name            StartAddress       EndAddress         Time
------------------- ------------------ ------------------ ----
dump_dumpfve.sys   0xfffff88001931000 0xfffff88001944000 2012-02-22 19:58:21
dump_atapi.sys     0xfffff88001928000 0xfffff88001931000 2012-02-22 19:58:21
dump_ataport.sys   0xfffff8800191c000 0xfffff88001928000 2012-02-22 19:58:21
crashdmp.sys       0xfffff8800190e000 0xfffff8800191c000 2012-02-22 19:58:21
```

2.3 PROCESSES AND DLLs

Once identified the correct profile, we can start to analyze the processes in the memory and, when the dump come from a windows system, the loaded DLLs.

2.3.1 pslist

To list the processes of a system, use the pslist command. This walks the doubly-linked list pointed to by **PsActiveProcessHead** and shows the offset, process name, process ID, the parent process ID, number of threads, number of handles, and date/time when the process started and exited.
As of 2.1 it also shows the Session ID and if the process is a Wow64 process (it uses a 32 bit address space on a 64 bit kernel).

This plugin does not detect hidden or unlinked processes (but **psscan** can do that).

If you see processes with 0 threads, 0 handles, and/or a non-empty exit time, the process may not actually still be active.

The Mis-leading 'Active' in **PsActiveProcessHead** and **ActiveProcessLinks** On Windows, the nt!PsActiveProcessHead symbol points to a doubly-linked list of EPROCESS objects. It is very well...mnin.blogspot.it

Below, you'll notice regsvr32.exe has terminated even though it's still in the "active" list.

Also note the two processes System and smss.exe will not have a Session ID, because System starts before sessions are established and smss.exe is the session manager itself.

```
$ vol.py -f win7.raw --profile=Win7SP0x64 pslist

Volatility Foundation Volatility Framework 2.6
Offset(V)        Name              PID  PPID  Thds   Hnds  Sess  Wow64 Start                Exit
----------------- ------------------ ------ ------ ------ -------- ------ ------ -------------------- ---------------
-----
0xfffffa80004b09e0 System             4    0    78    489 ------      0 2012-02-22 19:58:20
0xfffffa8000ce97f0 smss.exe          208    4    2     29 ------      0 2012-02-22 19:58:20
0xfffffa8000c006c0 csrss.exe         296  288    9    385    0        0 2012-02-22 19:58:24
0xfffffa8000c92300 wininit.exe       332  288    3     74    0        0 2012-02-22 19:58:30
0xfffffa8000c06b30 csrss.exe         344  324    7    252    1        0 2012-02-22 19:58:30
0xfffffa8000c80b30 winlogon.exe      372  324    5    136    1        0 2012-02-22 19:58:31
0xfffffa8000c5eb30 services.exe      428  332    6    193    0        0 2012-02-22 19:58:32
0xfffffa80011c5700 lsass.exe         444  332    6    557    0        0 2012-02-22 19:58:32
0xfffffa8000ea31b0 lsm.exe           452  332   10    133    0        0 2012-02-22 19:58:32
0xfffffa8001296b30 svchost.exe       568  428   10    352    0        0 2012-02-22 19:58:34
0xfffffa8001c3620 svchost.exe        628  428    6    247    0        0 2012-02-22 19:58:34
0xfffffa8001325950 sppsvc.exe        816  428    5    154    0        0 2012-02-22 19:58:41
0xfffffa80007b7960 svchost.exe       856  428   16    404    0        0 2012-02-22 19:58:43
0xfffffa80007bb750 svchost.exe       880  428   34   1118    0        0 2012-02-22 19:58:43
0xfffffa80007d09e0 svchost.exe       916  428   19    443    0        0 2012-02-22 19:58:43
0xfffffa8000c64840 svchost.exe       348  428   14    338    0        0 2012-02-22 20:02:07
0xfffffa8000c09630 svchost.exe       504  428   16    496    0        0 2012-02-22 20:02:07
0xfffffa8000e86690 spoolsv.exe      1076  428   12    271    0        0 2012-02-22 20:02:10
0xfffffa8000518b30 svchost.exe      1104  428   18    307    0        0 2012-02-22 20:02:10
0xfffffa800094d960 wlms.exe         1264  428    4     43    0        0 2012-02-22 20:02:11
0xfffffa8000995b30 svchost.exe      1736  428   12    200    0        0 2012-02-22 20:02:25
0xfffffa8000aa0b30 SearchIndexer.   1800  428   12    757    0        0 2012-02-22 20:02:26
0xfffffa8000aea630 taskhost.exe     1144  428    7    189    1        0 2012-02-22 20:02:41
0xfffffa8000eafb30 dwm.exe          1476  856    3     71    1        0 2012-02-22 20:02:41
0xfffffa80008f3420 explorer.exe     1652  840   21    760    1        0 2012-02-22 20:02:42
...
```

By default, pslist shows virtual offsets for the _EPROCESS but the physical offset can be obtained with the -P switch:

```
$ vol.py -f win7.raw --profile=Win7SP0x64 pslist -P

Volatility Foundation Volatility Framework 2.6
Offset(P)        Name              PID  PPID  Thds   Hnds  Sess  Wow64 Start                Exit
----------------- ------------------ ------ ------ ------ -------- ------ ------ -------------------- ---------------
-----
0x0000000017fef9e0 System             4    0    78    489 ------      0 2012-02-22 19:58:20
0x00000000176e97f0 smss.exe          208    4    2     29 ------      0 2012-02-22 19:58:20
0x00000000176006c0 csrss.exe         296  288    9    385    0        0 2012-02-22 19:58:24
0x0000000017692300 wininit.exe       332  288    3     74    0        0 2012-02-22 19:58:30
0x0000000017606b30 csrss.exe         344  324    7    252    1        0 2012-02-22 19:58:30
...
```

2.3.2   pstree

To view the process listing in tree form, use the **pstree** command. This enumerates processes using the same technique as pslist, so it will also not show hidden or unlinked processes. Child process are indicated using indention and periods.

```
$ vol.py -f win7.raw --profile=Win7SP0x64 pstree

Volatility Foundation Volatility Framework 2.6
Name                                    Pid   PPid  Thds  Hnds Time
--------------------------------------- ----- ----- ----- ----- --------------------
 0xffffffa80004b09e0:System                4     0    78   489 2012-02-22 19:58:20
. 0xffffffa8000ce97f0:smss.exe           208     4     2    29 2012-02-22 19:58:20
 0xffffffa8000c006c0:csrss.exe           296   288     9   385 2012-02-22 19:58:24
 0xffffffa8000c92300:wininit.exe         332   288     3    74 2012-02-22 19:58:30
. 0xffffffa8000c5eb30:services.exe       428   332     6   193 2012-02-22 19:58:32
.. 0xffffffa8000aa0b30:SearchIndexer.   1800   428    12   757 2012-02-22 20:02:26
.. 0xffffffa80007d09e0:svchost.exe       916   428    19   443 2012-02-22 19:58:43
.. 0xffffffa8000a4f630:svchost.exe      1432   428    12   350 2012-02-22 20:04:14
.. 0xffffffa800094d960:wlms.exe         1264   428     4    43 2012-02-22 20:02:11
.. 0xffffffa8001325950:sppsvc.exe        816   428     5   154 2012-02-22 19:58:41
.. 0xffffffa8000e86690:spoolsv.exe      1076   428    12   271 2012-02-22 20:02:10
.. 0xffffffa8001296b30:svchost.exe       568   428    10   352 2012-02-22 19:58:34
... 0xffffffa8000a03b30:rundll32.exe    2016   568     3    67 2012-02-22 20:03:16
...
```

2.3.3   psscan

To enumerate processes using pool tag scanning (_POOL_HEADER), use the psscan command.
This can find processes that previously terminated (inactive) and processes that have been hidden or unlinked by a rootkit. The downside is that rootkits can still hide by overwriting the pool tag values (though not commonly seen in the wild).

```
$ vol.py --profile=Win7SP0x86 -f win7.dmp psscan

Volatility Foundation Volatility Framework 2.0
Offset     Name            PID  PPID  PDB     Time created             Time exited
---------- --------------- ---- ----- ------- ------------------------ ------------------------
0x3e025ba8 svchost.exe     1116  508 0x3ecf1220 2010-06-16 15:25:25
0x3e04f070 svchost.exe     1152  508 0x3ecf1340 2010-06-16 15:27:40
0x3e144c08 dwm.exe         1540  832 0x3ecf12e0 2010-06-16 15:26:58
0x3e145c18 TPAutoConnSvc.  1900  508 0x3ecf1360 2010-06-16 15:25:41
0x3e3393f8 lsass.exe        516  392 0x3ecf10e0 2010-06-16 15:25:18
0x3e35b8f8 svchost.exe      628  508 0x3ecf1120 2010-06-16 15:25:19
0x3e383770 svchost.exe      832  508 0x3ecf11a0 2010-06-16 15:25:20
0x3e3949d0 svchost.exe      740  508 0x3ecf1160 2010-06-16 15:25:20
0x3e3a5100 svchost.exe      872  508 0x3ecf11c0 2010-06-16 15:25:20
0x3e3f64e8 svchost.exe      992  508 0x3ecf1200 2010-06-16 15:25:24
0x3e45a530 wininit.exe      392  316 0x3ecf10a0 2010-06-16 15:25:15
0x3e45d928 svchost.exe     1304  508 0x3ecf1260 2010-06-16 15:25:28
0x3e45f530 csrss.exe        400  384 0x3ecf1040 2010-06-16 15:25:15
0x3e4d89c8 vmtoolsd.exe    1436  508 0x3ecf1280 2010-06-16 15:25:30
0x3e4db030 spoolsv.exe     1268  508 0x3ecf1240 2010-06-16 15:25:28
0x3e50b318 services.exe     508  392 0x3ecf1080 2010-06-16 15:25:18
0x3e7f3d40 csrss.exe        352  316 0x3ecf1060 2010-06-16 15:25:12
0x3e7f5bc0 winlogon.exe     464  384 0x3ecf10c0 2010-06-16 15:25:18
0x3eac6030 SearchProtocol  2448 1168 0x3ecf15c0 2010-06-16 23:30:52   2010-06-16 23:33:14
...
```

If a process has previously terminated, the Time exited field will show the exit time. If you want to investigate a hidden process (such as displaying its DLLs), then you'll need physical offset of the _EPROCESS object, which is shown in the far left column.
Almost all process-related plugins take a --OFFSET parameter so that you can work with hidden processes.

2.3.4   psdispscan

This plugin is similar to psscan, except it enumerates processes by scanning for **DISPATCHER_HEADER** instead of pool tags. This gives you an alternate way to carve _EPROCESS objects in the event an attacker tried to hide by altering pool tags.

This plugin is not well maintained and only supports XP x86.
*To use it, you must type **--plugins=contrib/plugins** on command-line.*

2.3.5 dlllist and ldrmodules

To display a process's loaded DLLs, use the **dlllist** command. It walks the doubly-linked list of _LDR_DATA_TABLE_ENTRY structures which is pointed to by the PEB's InLoadOrderModuleList.

DLLs are automatically added to this list when a process calls LoadLibrary (or some derivative such as LdrLoadDll) and they aren't removed until FreeLibrary is called and the reference count reaches zero.

The load count column tells you if a DLL was statically loaded (i.e. as a result of being in the exe or another DLL's import table) or dynamically loaded.

```
$ vol.py -f win7.raw --profile=Win7SP0x64 dlllist

****************************************************************************
wininit.exe pid:    332
Command line : wininit.exe

Base                Size            LoadCount Path
----------------    --------------- ----------------- ----
0x00000000ff530000      0x23000         0xffff C:\Windows\system32\wininit.exe
0x0000000076d40000      0x1ab000        0xffff C:\Windows\SYSTEM32\ntdll.dll
0x0000000076b20000      0x11f000        0xffff C:\Windows\system32\kernel32.dll
0x000007fefcd50000      0x6b000         0xffff C:\Windows\system32\KERNELBASE.dll
0x0000000076c40000      0xfa000         0xffff C:\Windows\system32\USER32.dll
0x000007fefd7c0000      0x67000         0xffff C:\Windows\system32\GDI32.dll
0x000007fefe190000      0xe000          0xffff C:\Windows\system32\LPK.dll
0x000007fefef80000      0xca000         0xffff C:\Windows\system32\USP10.dll
0x000007fefd860000      0x9f000         0xffff C:\Windows\system32\msvcrt.dll
...
```

To display the DLLs for a specific process instead of all processes, use the -por --pid filter as shown below.

Also, in the following output, notice we're analyzing a Wow64 process. Wow64 processes have a limited list of DLLs in the PEB lists, but that doesn't mean they're the *only* DLLs loaded in the process address space.

Thus Volatility will remind you to use the **ldrmodules** instead for these processes.

```
$ vol.py -f win7.raw --profile=Win7SP0x64 dlllist -p 1892

Volatility Foundation Volatility Framework 2.6
*******************************************************************
iexplore.exe pid:   1892
Command line : "C:\Program Files (x86)\Internet Explorer\iexplore.exe"
Note: use ldrmodules for listing DLLs in Wow64 processes

Base               Size              LoadCount Path
------------------ ----------------- ------------------- ----
0x0000000000080000       0xa6000          0xffff C:\Program Files (x86)\Internet
Explorer\iexplore.exe
0x0000000076d40000       0x1ab000         0xffff C:\Windows\SYSTEM32\ntdll.dll
0x00000000748d0000       0x3f000          0x3 C:\Windows\SYSTEM32\wow64.dll
0x0000000074870000       0x5c000          0x1 C:\Windows\SYSTEM32\wow64win.dll
0x0000000074940000       0x8000           0x1 C:\Windows\SYSTEM32\wow64cpu.dll
```

To display the DLLs for a process that is hidden or unlinked by a rootkit, first use the psscan to get the physical offset of the EPROCESS object and supply it with **--offset=OFFSET**.

The plugin will "bounce back" and determine the virtual address of the EPROCESS and then acquire an address space in order to access the PEB.

```
$ vol.py -f win7.raw --profile=Win7SP0x64 dlllist --offset=0x04a291a8
```

2.3.6   dlldump

To extract a DLL from a process's memory space and dump it to disk for analysis, use the dlldump command.

The syntax is nearly the same as what we've shown for dlllist above. You can:

- Dump all DLLs from all processes
- Dump all DLLs from a specific process (with --pid=PID)
- Dump all DLLs from a hidden/unlinked process (with --offset=OFFSET)
- Dump a PE from anywhere in process memory (with --base=BASEADDR), this option is useful for extracting hidden DLLs
- Dump one or more DLLs that match a regular expression (--regex=REGEX), case sensitive or not (--ignore-case)

To specify an output directory, use **--dump-dir=DIR** or -d DIR.

```
$ vol.py -f win7.raw --profile=Win7SP0x64 dlldump -D dlls/

...
Process(V)        Name              Module Base       Module Name        Result
------------------ ------------------ ------------------- -------------------- ------
0xfffffa8000ce97f0 smss.exe          0x0000000047a90000 smss.exe           OK: module.208.176e97f0.47a90000.dll
0xfffffa8000ce97f0 smss.exe          0x0000000076d40000                    Error: DllBase is paged
0xfffffa8000c006c0 csrss.exe         0x0000000049700000 csrss.exe          OK: module.296.176006c0.49700000.dll
0xfffffa8000c006c0 csrss.exe         0x0000000076d40000 ntdll.dll          Error: DllBase is paged
0xfffffa8000c006c0 csrss.exe         0x00007fefd860000 msvcrt.dll         Error: DllBase is paged
0xfffffa80011c5700 lsass.exe         0x00007fefcc40000 WINSTA.dll         Error: DllBase is paged
0xfffffa80011c5700 lsass.exe         0x00007fefd7c0000 GDI32.dll          OK: module.444.173c5700.7fefd7c0000.dll
0xfffffa80011c5700 lsass.exe         0x00007fefc270000 DNSAPI.dll         OK: module.444.173c5700.7fefc270000.dll
0xfffffa80011c5700 lsass.exe         0x00007fefc5d0000 Secur32.dll        OK: module.444.173c5700.7fefc5d0000.dll
...
```

If the extraction fails, as it did for a few DLLs above, it probably means that some of the memory pages in that DLL were not memory resident (due to paging). In particular, this is a problem if the first page containing the PE header and thus the PE section mappings is not available.

To dump a PE file that doesn't exist in the DLLs list (for example, due to code injection or malicious unlinking), just specify the base address of the PE in process memory:

```
$ vol.py --profile=Win7SP0x86 -f win7.dmp dlldump --pid=492 -D out --
base=0x00680000
```

You can also specify an EPROCESS offset if the DLL you want is in a hidden process:

```
$ vol.py --profile=Win7SP0x86 -f win7.dmp dlldump -o 0x3e3f64e8 -D out --
base=0x00680000
```

2.3.7   Handles

To display the open handles in a process, use the handles command. This applies to files, registry keys, mutexes, named pipes, events, window stations, desktops, threads, and all other types of securable executive objects.

```
$ vol.py -f win7.raw --profile=Win7SP0x64 handles

Volatility Foundation Volatility Framework 2.6
Offset(V)          Pid        Handle           Access Type         Details
------------------ ------ ------------------ ------------------ ---------------- -------
0xfffffa80004b09e0     4          0x4        0x1fffff Process      System(4)
0xfffff8a0000821a0     4          0x10       0x2001f Key
MACHINE\SYSTEM\CONTROLSET001\CONTROL\PRODUCTOPTIONS
0xfffff8a00007e040     4          0x14       0xf003f Key
MACHINE\SYSTEM\CONTROLSET001\CONTROL\SESSION MANAGER\MEMORY
MANAGEMENT\PREFETCHPARAMETERS
0xfffff8a000081fa0     4          0x18       0x2001f Key          MACHINE\SYSTEM\SETUP
0xfffff8000546990      4          0x1c       0x1f0001 ALPC Port   PowerMonitorPort
0xfffff800054d070      4          0x20       0x1f0001 ALPC Port   PowerPort
0xfffff8a0000676a0     4          0x24       0x20019 Key
MACHINE\HARDWARE\DESCRIPTION\SYSTEM\MULTIFUNCTIONADAPTER
0xfffff8000625460      4          0x28       0x1fffff Thread      TID 160 PID 4
0xfffff8a00007f400     4          0x2c       0xf003f Key          MACHINE\SYSTEM\CONTROLSET001
0xfffff8a00007f200     4          0x30       0xf003f Key
MACHINE\SYSTEM\CONTROLSET001\ENUM
0xfffff8a000080d10     4          0x34       0xf003f Key
MACHINE\SYSTEM\CONTROLSET001\CONTROL\CLASS
0xfffff8a00007f500     4          0x38       0xf003f Key
MACHINE\SYSTEM\CONTROLSET001\SERVICES
0xfffff8a0001cd990     4          0x3c       0xe Token
0xfffff8a00007bfa0     4          0x40       0x20019 Key
MACHINE\SYSTEM\CONTROLSET001\CONTROL\WMI\SECURITY
0xfffffa8000cd52b0     4          0x44       0x120116 File        \Device\Mup
0xfffffa8000ce97f0     4          0x48       0x2a Process         smss.exe(208)
0xfffffa8000df16f0     4          0x4c       0x120089 File
\Device\HarddiskVolume2\Windows\System32\en-US\win32k.sys.mui
0xfffff8000de37f0      4          0x50       0x12019f File        \Device\clfsTxfLog
0xfffff8a000952fa0     4          0x54       0x2001f Key
MACHINE\SYSTEM\CONTROLSET001\CONTROL\VIDEO\{6A8FC9DC-A76B-47FC-A703-
17800182E1CE}\0000\VOLATILESETTINGS
0xfffff800078da20      4          0x58       0x12019f File        \Device\Tcp
0xfffff8a002e17610     4          0x5c       0x9 Key
MACHINE\SOFTWARE\MICROSOFT\WINDOWS NT\CURRENTVERSION\IMAGE FILE EXECUTION OPTIONS
0xfffff8a0008f7b00     4          0x60       0x10 Key
MACHINE\SYSTEM\CONTROLSET001\CONTROL\LSA
0xfffffa8000da2870     4          0x64       0x100001 File        \Device\KsecDD
0xfffffa8000da3040     4          0x68       0x0 Thread           TID 228 PID 4
...
```

You can display handles for a particular process by specifying --pid=PID or the physical offset of an _EPROCESS structure (--physical-offset=OFFSET). You can also filter by object type using -t or --object-type=OBJECTTYPE.

For example to only display handles to process objects for pid 600, do the following:

```
$ vol.py -f win7.raw --profile=Win7SP0x64 handles -p 296 -t Process
Volatility Foundation Volatility Framework 2.6
Offset(V)            Pid          Handle          Access Type         Details
------------------ ------ ------------------ -------------------- ---------------- -------
0xfffffa8000c92300   296          0x54         0x1fffff Process       wininit.exe(332)
0xfffffa8000c5eb30   296          0xc4         0x1fffff Process       services.exe(428)
0xfffffa80011c5700   296          0xd4         0x1fffff Process       lsass.exe(444)
0xfffffa8000ea31b0   296          0xe4         0x1fffff Process       lsm.exe(452)
0xfffffa8000c64840   296          0x140        0x1fffff Process       svchost.exe(348)
0xfffffa8001296b30   296          0x150        0x1fffff Process       svchost.exe(568)
0xfffffa80012c3620   296          0x18c        0x1fffff Process       svchost.exe(628)
...
```

The object type can be any of the names printed by the "object \ObjectTypes" windbg command.

In some cases, the Details column will be blank (for example, if the objects don't have names).

By default, you'll see both named and un-named objects.

However, if you want to hide the less meaningful results and only show named objects, use the **--silent** parameter to this plugin.

2.3.8   getsids

To view the **SIDs (Security Identifiers)** associated with a process, use the getsids command.
Among other things, this can help you identify processes which have maliciously escalated privileges and which processes belong to specific users.

```
$ vol.py -f win7.raw --profile=Win7SP0x64 getsids

Volatility Foundation Volatility Framework 2.6
System (4): S-1-5-18 (Local System)
System (4): S-1-5-32-544 (Administrators)
System (4): S-1-1-0 (Everyone)
System (4): S-1-5-11 (Authenticated Users)
System (4): S-1-16-16384 (System Mandatory Level)
smss.exe (208): S-1-5-18 (Local System)
smss.exe (208): S-1-5-32-544 (Administrators)
smss.exe (208): S-1-1-0 (Everyone)
smss.exe (208): S-1-5-11 (Authenticated Users)
smss.exe (208): S-1-16-16384 (System Mandatory Level)
...
```

2.3.9   cmdscan

The cmdscan plugin searches the memory of csrss.exe on XP/2003/Vista/2008 and conhost.exe on Windows 7 for commands that attackers entered through a console shell (cmd.exe).

This is one of the most powerful commands you can use to gain visibility into an attackers actions on a victim system, whether they opened cmd.exe through an RDP session or proxied input/output to a command shell from a networked backdoor.

This plugin finds structures known as COMMAND_HISTORY by looking for a known constant value (MaxHistory) and then applying sanity checks. It is important to note that the MaxHistory value can be changed by right clicking in the top left of a cmd.exe window and going to Properties. The value can also be changed for all consoles opened by a given user by modifying the registry key **HKCU\Console\HistoryBufferSize**.

The default is 50 on Windows systems, meaning the most recent 50 commands are saved.

You can tweak it if needed by using the **--max_history=NUMBER** parameter.

The structures used by this plugin are not public (i.e. Microsoft does not produce PDBs for them), thus they're not available in WinDBG or any other forensic framework.
They were reverse engineered by Michael Ligh from the conhost.exe and winsrv.dll binaries.

In addition to the commands entered into a shell, this plugin shows:

- The name of the console host process (csrss.exe or conhost.exe)
- The name of the application using the console (whatever process is using cmd.exe)

- The location of the command history buffers, including the current buffer count, last added command, and last displayed command
- The application process handle

Due to the scanning technique this plugin uses, it has the capability to find commands from both active and closed consoles.

```
$ vol.py -f VistaSP2x64.vmem --profile=VistaSP2x64 cmdscan

Volatility Foundation Volatility Framework 2.6

**************************************************
CommandProcess: csrss.exe Pid: 528
CommandHistory: 0x135ec00 Application: cmd.exe Flags: Allocated, Reset
CommandCount: 18 LastAdded: 17 LastDisplayed: 17
FirstCommand: 0 CommandCountMax: 50
ProcessHandle: 0x330
Cmd #0 @ 0x135ef10: cd \
Cmd #1 @ 0x135ef50: cd de
Cmd #2 @ 0x135ef70: cd PerfLogs
Cmd #3 @ 0x135ef90: cd ..
Cmd #4 @ 0x5c78b90: cd "Program Files"
Cmd #5 @ 0x135fae0: cd "Debugging Tools for Windows (x64)"
Cmd #6 @ 0x135efb0: livekd -w
Cmd #7 @ 0x135f010: windbg
Cmd #8 @ 0x135efd0: cd \
Cmd #9 @ 0x135fd20: rundll32 c:\apphelp.dll,ExportFunc
Cmd #10 @ 0x5c8bdb0: rundll32 c:\windows_apphelp.dll,ExportFunc
Cmd #11 @ 0x5c8be10: rundll32 c:\windows_apphelp.dll
Cmd #12 @ 0x135ee30: rundll32 c:\windows_apphelp.dll,Test
Cmd #13 @ 0x135fd70: cd "Program Files"
Cmd #14 @ 0x5c8b9e0: dir
Cmd #15 @ 0x5c8be60: cd "Debugging Tools for Windows (x64)"
Cmd #16 @ 0x5c8ba00: dir
Cmd #17 @ 0x135eff0: livekd –w
...
```

2.3.10 consoles

Similar to cmdscan the consoles plugin finds commands that attackers typed into cmd.exe or executed via backdoors. However, instead of scanning for COMMAND_HISTORY, this plugin scans for CONSOLE_INFORMATION.

The major advantage to this plugin is it not only prints the commands attackers typed, but it collects the entire screen buffer (input **and** output). For instance, instead of just seeing "dir", you'll see exactly what the attacker saw, including all files and directories listed by the "dir" command.

Additionally, this plugin prints the following:

- The original console window title and current console window title
- The name and pid of attached processes (walks a LIST_ENTRY to enumerate all of them if more than one)
- Any aliases associated with the commands executed. For example, attackers can register an alias such that typing "hello" actually executes "cd system"
- The screen coordinates of the cmd.exe console

Here's an example of the consoles command. Below, you'll notice something quite funny. The forensic investigator seems to have lost his mind and cannot find the dd.exe tool for dumping memory. Nearly 20 typos later, he finds the tool and uses it.

```
$ vol.py -f xp-laptop-2005-07-04-1430.img consoles

Volatility Foundation Volatility Framework 2.6

[csrss.exe @ 0x821c11a8 pid 456 console @ 0x4e23b0]
  OriginalTitle: '%SystemRoot%\\system32\\cmd.exe'
  Title: 'C:\\WINDOWS\\system32\\cmd.exe - dd if=\\\\.\\PhysicalMemory of=c:\\xp-2005-07-04-
1430.img conv=noerror'
  HistoryBufferCount: 2
  HistoryBufferMax: 4
  CommandHistorySize: 50
[history @ 0x4e4008]
  CommandCount: 0
  CommandCountMax: 50
  Application: 'dd.exe'
```

```
[history @ 0x4e4d88]
  CommandCount: 20
  CommandCountMax: 50
  Application: 'cmd.exe'
  Cmd #0 @ 0x4e1f90: 'dd'
  Cmd #1 @ 0x4e2cb8: 'cd\\'
  Cmd #2 @ 0x4e2d18: 'dr'
  Cmd #3 @ 0x4e2d28: 'ee:'
  Cmd #4 @ 0x4e2d38: 'e;'
  Cmd #5 @ 0x4e2d48: 'e:'
  Cmd #6 @ 0x4e2d58: 'dr'
  Cmd #7 @ 0x4e2d68: 'd;'
  Cmd #8 @ 0x4e2d78: 'd:'
  Cmd #9 @ 0x4e2d88: 'dr'
  Cmd #10 @ 0x4e2d98: 'ls'
  Cmd #11 @ 0x4e2da8: 'cd Docu'
  Cmd #12 @ 0x4e2dc0: 'cd Documents and'
  Cmd #13 @ 0x4e2e58: 'dr'
  Cmd #14 @ 0x4e2e68: 'd:'
  Cmd #15 @ 0x4e2e78: 'cd dd\\'
  Cmd #16 @ 0x4e2e90: 'cd UnicodeRelease'
  Cmd #17 @ 0x4e2ec0: 'dr'
  Cmd #18 @ 0x4e2ed0: 'dd '
  Cmd #19 @ 0x4e4100: 'dd if=\\\\.\\PhysicalMemory of=c:\\xp-2005-07-04-1430.img conv=noerror'
[screen @ 0x4e2460 X:80 Y:300]
  Output: Microsoft Windows XP [Version 5.1.2600]
  Output: (C) Copyright 1985-2001 Microsoft Corp.
  Output:
  Output: C:\Documents and Settings\Sarah>dd
  Output: 'dd' is not recognized as an internal or external command,
  Output: operable program or batch file.
  Output:
  Output: C:\Documents and Settings\Sarah>cd\
  Output:
  Output: C:\>dr
  Output: 'dr' is not recognized as an internal or external command,
  Output: operable program or batch file.
  Output:
  Output: C:\>ee:
  Output: 'ee:' is not recognized as an internal or external command,
  Output: operable program or batch file.
  Output:
  Output: C:\>e;
  Output: 'e' is not recognized as an internal or external command,
  Output: operable program or batch file.
  Output:
  Output: C:\>e:
  Output: The system cannot find the drive specified.
  Output:
  Output: C:\>dr
  Output: 'dr' is not recognized as an internal or external command,
  Output: operable program or batch file.
  Output:
  Output: C:\>d;
  Output: 'd' is not recognized as an internal or external command,
  Output: operable program or batch file.
  Output:
  Output: C:\>d:
  Output:
  Output: D:\>dr
  Output: 'dr' is not recognized as an internal or external command,
  Output: operable program or batch file.
  Output:
  Output: D:\>dr
  Output: 'dr' is not recognized as an internal or external command,
  Output: operable program or batch file.
  Output:
  Output: D:\>ls
```

```
Output: 'ls' is not recognized as an internal or external command,
Output: operable program or batch file.
Output:
Output: D:\>cd Docu
Output: The system cannot find the path specified.
Output:
Output: D:\>cd Documents and
Output: The system cannot find the path specified.
Output:
Output: D:\>dr
Output: 'dr' is not recognized as an internal or external command,
Output: operable program or batch file.
Output:
Output: D:\>d:
Output:
Output: D:\>cd dd\
Output:
Output: D:\dd>
Output: D:\dd>cd UnicodeRelease
Output:
Output: D:\dd\UnicodeRelease>dr
Output: 'dr' is not recognized as an internal or external command,
Output: operable program or batch file.
Output:
Output: D:\dd\UnicodeRelease>dd
Output:
Output: 0+0 records in
Output: 0+0 records out
Output: ^C
Output: D:\dd\UnicodeRelease>dd if=\\.\PhysicalMemory of=c:\xp-2005-07-04-1430.img conv=
Output: noerror
Output: Forensic Acquisition Utilities, 1, 0, 0, 1035
Output: dd, 3, 16, 2, 1035
Output: Copyright (C) 2002-2004 George M. Garner Jr.
Output:
Output: Command Line: dd if=\\.\PhysicalMemory of=c:\xp-2005-07-04-1430.img conv=noerror
Output:
Output: Based on original version developed by Paul Rubin, David MacKenzie, and Stuart K
Output: emp
Output: Microsoft Windows: Version 5.1 (Build 2600.Professional Service Pack 2)
Output:
Output: 04/07/2005  18:30:32 (UTC)
Output: 04/07/2005  14:30:32 (local time)
Output:
Output: Current User: SPLATITUDE\Sarah
Output:
Output: Total physical memory reported: 523676 KB
Output: Copying physical memory...
Output: Physical memory in the range 0x00004000-0x00004000 could not be read.
```

2.3.11 privs

This plugin shows you which process privileges are present, enabled, and/or enabled by default. You can pass it the **--silent** flag to only show privileges that a process explicitly enabled (i.e. that were were not enabled by default but are currently enabled).

The **--regex=REGEX** parameter can be used to filter for specific privilege names.

```
$ vol.py -f win7.raw privs --profile=Win7SP0x64
```

Volatility Foundation Volatility Framework 2.6

Pid	Process	Value	Privilege	Attributes	Description
4	System	2	SeCreateTokenPrivilege	Present	Create a token object
4	System	3	SeAssignPrimaryTokenPrivilege	Present	Replace a process-level token
4	System	4	SeLockMemoryPrivilege	Present,Enabled,Default	Lock pages in memory
4	System	5	SeIncreaseQuotaPrivilege	Present	Increase quotas
4	System	6	SeMachineAccountPrivilege		Add workstations to the domain
4	System	7	SeTcbPrivilege	Present,Enabled,Default	Act as part of the operating system
4	System	8	SeSecurityPrivilege	Present	Manage auditing and security log
4	System	9	SeTakeOwnershipPrivilege	Present	Take ownership of files/objects
4	System	10	SeLoadDriverPrivilege	Present	Load and unload device drivers
4	System	11	SeSystemProfilePrivilege	Present,Enabled,Default	Profile system performance
4	System	12	SeSystemtimePrivilege	Present	Change the system time
4	System	13	SeProfileSingleProcessPrivilege	Present,Enabled,Default	Profile a single process
4	System	14	SeIncreaseBasePriorityPrivilege	Present,Enabled,Default	Increase scheduling priority
4	System	15	SeCreatePagefilePrivilege	Present,Enabled,Default	Create a pagefile
4	System	16	SeCreatePermanentPrivilege	Present,Enabled,Default	Create permanent shared objects

.....

2.3.12 envars

To display a process's environment variables, use the envars plugin. Typically this will show the number of CPUs installed and the hardware architecture (though the **kdbgscan** output is a much more reliable source), the process's current directory, temporary directory, session name, computer name, user name, and various other interesting artifacts.

$ vol.py -f win7.raw --profile=Win7SP0x64 envars

```
Volatility Foundation Volatility Framework 2.6
Pid     Process            Block              Variable                      Value
-------- ------------------ ------------------ ----------------------------- -----
   296 csrss.exe           0x00000000003d1320 ComSpec              C:\Windows\system32\cmd.exe
   296 csrss.exe           0x00000000003d1320 FP_NO_HOST_CHECK             NO
   296 csrss.exe           0x00000000003d1320 NUMBER_OF_PROCESSORS       1
   296 csrss.exe           0x00000000003d1320 OS                  Windows_NT
   296 csrss.exe           0x00000000003d1320 Path
C:\Windows\system32;C:\Windows;C:\Windows\System32\Wbem;C:\Windows\System32\WindowsPower
Shell\v1.0\
   296 csrss.exe           0x00000000003d1320 PATHEXT
.COM;.EXE;.BAT;.CMD;.VBS;.VBE;.JS;.JSE;.WSF;.WSH;.MSC
   296 csrss.exe           0x00000000003d1320 PROCESSOR_ARCHITECTURE       AMD64
   296 csrss.exe           0x00000000003d1320 PROCESSOR_IDENTIFIER       Intel64 Family 6 Model 2
Stepping 3, GenuineIntel
   296 csrss.exe           0x00000000003d1320 PROCESSOR_LEVEL           6
   296 csrss.exe           0x00000000003d1320 PROCESSOR_REVISION        0203
   296 csrss.exe           0x00000000003d1320 PSModulePath
C:\Windows\system32\WindowsPowerShell\v1.0\Modules\
   296 csrss.exe           0x00000000003d1320 SystemDrive          C:
   296 csrss.exe           0x00000000003d1320 SystemRoot           C:\Windows
   296 csrss.exe           0x00000000003d1320 TEMP                 C:\Windows\TEMP
   296 csrss.exe           0x00000000003d1320 TMP                  C:\Windows\TEMP
   296 csrss.exe           0x00000000003d1320 USERNAME             SYSTEM
   296 csrss.exe           0x00000000003d1320 windir               C:\Windows
```

2.3.13 verinfo

To display the version information embedded in PE files, use the **verinfo** command.
Not all PE files have version information, and many malware authors forge it to include false data, but nonetheless this command can be very helpful with identifying binaries and for making correlations with other files.

This plugin only supports printing version information from process executables and DLLs, but later will be expanded to include kernel modules. If you want to filter by module name, use the — regex=REGEX and/or — ignore-case options.

```
$ vol.py -f win7.raw --profile=Win7SP0x64 verinfo
Volatility Foundation Volatility Framework 2.6
\SystemRoot\System32\smss.exe
C:\Windows\SYSTEM32\ntdll.dll

C:\Windows\system32\csrss.exe
  File version   : 6.1.7600.16385
  Product version : 6.1.7600.16385
  Flags    :
  OS         : Windows NT
  File Type    : Application
  File Date    :
  CompanyName : Microsoft Corporation
  FileDescription : Client Server Runtime Process
  FileVersion : 6.1.7600.16385 (win7_rtm.090713-1255)
  InternalName : CSRSS.Exe
  LegalCopyright : \xa9 Microsoft Corporation. All rights reserved.
  OriginalFilename : CSRSS.Exe
  ProductName : Microsoft\xae Windows\xae Operating System
  ProductVersion : 6.1.7600.16385

...
```

2.3.14 enumfunc

This plugin enumerates imported and exported functions from processes, dlls, and kernel drivers. Specifically, it handles functions imported by name or ordinal, functions exported by name or ordinal, and forwarded exports.
The output will be very verbose in most cases (functions exported by ntdll, msvcrt, and kernel32 can reach 1000+ alone).

So you can either reduce the verbosity by filtering criteria with the command-line options (shown below) or you can use look at the code in enumfunc.py and use it as an example of how to use the IAT and EAT parsing API functions in your own plugin.
For example, the apihooks plugin leverages the imports and exports APIs to find functions in memory when checking for hooks.

Also note this plugin is in the contrib directory, so you can pass that to --plugins like this:

```
$ vol.py --plugins=contrib/plugins/ -f win7.raw --profile=Win7SP0x64
enumfunc -h
....
 -s, --scan          Scan for objects
 -P, --process-only  Process only
 -K, --kernel-only   Kernel only
 -I, --import-only   Imports only
 -E, --export-only   Exports only
```

To use pool scanners for finding processes and kernel drivers instead of walking linked lists, use the -s option. This can be useful if you're trying to enumerate functions in hidden processes or drivers. An example of the remaining command-line options is shown below.

To show exported functions in process memory, use -P and -E like this:

```
$ vol.py --plugins=contrib/plugins/ -f win7.raw --profile=Win7SP0x64 enumfunc -P -E
```

Process	Type	Module	Ordinal	Address	Name
lsass.exe	Export	ADVAPI32.dll	1133	0x000007fefd11dd34	CreateWellKnownSid
lsass.exe	Export	ADVAPI32.dll	1134	0x000007fefd17a460	CredBackupCredentials
lsass.exe	Export	ADVAPI32.dll	1135	0x000007fefd170590	CredDeleteA
lsass.exe	Export	ADVAPI32.dll	1136	0x000007fefd1704d0	CredDeleteW
lsass.exe	Export	ADVAPI32.dll	1137	0x000007fefd17a310	
CredEncryptAndMarshalBinaryBlob					
lsass.exe	Export	ADVAPI32.dll	1138	0x000007fefd17d080	CredEnumerateA
lsass.exe	Export	ADVAPI32.dll	1139	0x000007fefd17cf50	CredEnumerateW
lsass.exe	Export	ADVAPI32.dll	1140	0x000007fefd17ca00	CredFindBestCredentialA
lsass.exe	Export	ADVAPI32.dll	1141	0x000007fefd17c8f0	CredFindBestCredentialW
lsass.exe	Export	ADVAPI32.dll	1142	0x000007fefd130c10	CredFree
lsass.exe	Export	ADVAPI32.dll	1143	0x000007fefd1630f0	CredGetSessionTypes
lsass.exe	Export	ADVAPI32.dll	1144	0x000007fefd1703d0	CredGetTargetInfoA

...

To show imported functions in kernel memory, use -K and -I like this:

```
$ vol.py --plugins=contrib/plugins/ -f win7.raw --profile=Win7SP0x64 enumfunc -K -I
```

Volatility Foundation Volatility Framework 2.6

Process	Type	Module	Ordinal	Address	Name
<KERNEL>	Import	VIDEOPRT.SYS	583	0xfffff80002acc320	
ntoskrnl.exeIoRegisterPlugPlayNotification					
<KERNEL>	Import	VIDEOPRT.SYS	1325	0xfffff800029f9f30	
ntoskrnl.exeRtlAppendStringToString					
<KERNEL>	Import	VIDEOPRT.SYS	509	0xfffff800026d06e0	
ntoskrnl.exeIoGetAttachedDevice					
<KERNEL>	Import	VIDEOPRT.SYS	443	0xfffff800028f7ec0	
ntoskrnl.exeIoBuildSynchronousFsdRequest					
<KERNEL>	Import	VIDEOPRT.SYS	1466	0xfffff80002699300	
ntoskrnl.exeRtlInitUnicodeString					
<KERNEL>	Import	VIDEOPRT.SYS	759	0xfffff80002697be0	
ntoskrnl.exeKeInitializeEvent					
<KERNEL>	Import	VIDEOPRT.SYS	1461	0xfffff8000265e8a0	
ntoskrnl.exeRtlInitAnsiString					
<KERNEL>	Import	VIDEOPRT.SYS	1966	0xfffff80002685060	
ntoskrnl.exeZwSetValueKey					
<KERNEL>	Import	VIDEOPRT.SYS	840	0xfffff80002699440	
ntoskrnl.exeKeReleaseSpinLock					
<KERNEL>	Import	VIDEOPRT.SYS	1190	0xfffff800027a98b0	
ntoskrnl.exePoRequestPowerIrp					
<KERNEL>	Import	VIDEOPRT.SYS	158	0xfffff800026840f0	
ntoskrnl.exeExInterlockedInsertTailList					
<KERNEL>	Import	VIDEOPRT.SYS	1810	0xfffff80002684640	ntoskrnl.exeZwClose

...

2.4 PROCESS MEMORY

If we try to analyze the memory more thoroughly, without focusing only on the processes, we can find other interesting information.

2.4.1 memmap

The memmap command shows you exactly which pages are memory resident, given a specific process DTB (or kernel DTB if you use this plugin on the Idle or System process). It shows you the virtual address of the page, the corresponding physical offset of the page, and the size of the page. The map information generated by this plugin comes from the underlying address space's get_available_addresses method.

The column DumpFileOffset helps you correlate the output of memmap with the dump file produced by the memdump plugin. For example, according to the output below, the page at virtual address 0x0000000000058000 in the System process's memory can be found at offset 0x00000000162ed000 of the win7.raw file. After using memdump to extract the addressable memory of the System process to an individual file, you can find this page at offset 0x8000.

```
$ vol.py -f win7.raw --profile=Win7SP0x64 memmap -p 4

Volatility Foundation Volatility Framework 2.6
System pid:    4
Virtual          Physical              Size    DumpFileOffset
---------------- ------------------ ------------------ ------------------
0x0000000000050000 0x0000000000cbc000      0x1000         0x0
0x0000000000051000 0x0000000015ec6000      0x1000       0x1000
0x0000000000052000 0x000000000f5e7000      0x1000       0x2000
0x0000000000053000 0x0000000005e28000      0x1000       0x3000
0x0000000000054000 0x0000000008b29000      0x1000       0x4000
0x0000000000055000 0x00000000155b8000      0x1000       0x5000
0x0000000000056000 0x000000000926e000      0x1000       0x6000
0x0000000000057000 0x0000000002dac000      0x1000       0x7000
0x0000000000058000 0x00000000162ed000      0x1000       0x8000
...
```

2.4.2   memdump

To extract all memory resident pages in a process (see memmap for details) into an individual file, use the memdump command.

Supply the output directory with -D or — dump-dir=DIR.

```
$ vol.py -f win7.raw --profile=Win7SP0x64 memdump -p 4 -D dump/

Volatility Foundation Volatility Framework 2.6
***************************************************************************
Writing System [     4] to 4.dmp

$ ls -alh dump/4.dmp
-rw-r--r--  1 Michael  staff    111M Jun 24 15:47 dump/4.dmp

To conclude the demonstration we began in the memmap discussion, we should now be able to make an
assertion regarding the relationship of the mapped and extracted pages:

$ vol.py -f ~/Desktop/win7.raw --profile=Win7SP0x64 volshell
Volatility Foundation Volatility Framework 2.6
Current context: process System, pid=4, ppid=0 DTB=0x187000
Welcome to volshell Current memory image is:
file:///Users/Michael/Desktop/win7.raw
To get help, type 'hh()'

>>> PAGE_SIZE = 0x1000

>>> assert addrspace().read(0x0000000000058000, PAGE_SIZE) == \
...      addrspace().base.read(0x00000000162ed000, PAGE_SIZE) == \
...      open("dump/4.dmp", "rb").read()[0x8000:0x8000 + PAGE_SIZE]
>>>
```

2.4.3   procdump

To dump a process's executable, use the procdump command.
Optionally, pass the --unsafe or -u flags to bypass certain sanity checks
used when parsing the PE header. Some malware will intentionally forge
size fields in the PE header so that memory dumping tools fail.

Use --memory to include slack space between the PE sections that
aren't page aligned. Without --memory you'll get a file that more closely
resembles the file on disk, before sections expanded.

```
$ vol.py -f win7.raw --profile=Win7SP0x64 procdump -D dump/ -p 296

Volatility Foundation Volatility Framework 2.6
*********************************************************************
Dumping csrss.exe, pid:    296 output: executable.296.exe

$ file dump/executable.296.exe
dump/executable.296.exe: PE32+ executable for MS Windows (native) Mono/.Net assembly
```

2.4.4   vadinfo

The vadinfo command displays extended information about a process's VAD nodes. In particular, it shows:

- The address of the MMVAD structure in kernel memory
- The starting and ending virtual addresses in process memory that the MMVAD structure pertains to
- The VAD Tag
- The VAD flags, control flags, etc
- The name of the memory mapped file (if one exists)
- The memory protection constant (permissions). Note there is a difference between the original protection and current protection. The original protection is derived from the flProtect parameter to VirtualAlloc. For example you can reserve memory (MEM_RESERVE) with protection PAGE_NOACCESS (original protection). Later, you can call VirtualAlloc again to commit (MEM_COMMIT) and specify PAGE_READWRITE (becomes current protection). The vadinfo command shows the original protection only. Thus, just because you see PAGE_NOACCESS here, it doesn't mean code in the region cannot be read, written, or executed.

```
$ vol.py -f win7.raw --profile=Win7SP0x64 vadinfo -p 296
Volatility Foundation Volatility Framework 2.6
****************************************************************************
Pid:    296
VAD node @ 0xfffffa8000c00620 Start 0x000000007f0e0000 End 0x000000007ffdffff Tag VadS
Flags: PrivateMemory: 1, Protection: 1
Protection: PAGE_READONLY
Vad Type: VadNone

[snip]

VAD node @ 0xfffffa8000c04ce0 Start 0x000007fefcd00000 End 0x000007fefcd10fff Tag Vad
Flags: CommitCharge: 2, Protection: 7, VadType: 2
Protection: PAGE_EXECUTE_WRITECOPY
Vad Type: VadImageMap
ControlArea @fffffa8000c04d70 Segment fffff8a000c45c10
Dereference list: Flink 00000000, Blink 00000000
NumberOfSectionReferences:          0 NumberOfPfnReferences:        13
NumberOfMappedViews:                2 NumberOfUserReferences:       2
WaitingForDeletion Event: 00000000
Control Flags: Accessed: 1, File: 1, Image: 1
FileObject @fffffa8000c074d0, Name: \Windows\System32\basesrv.dll
First prototype PTE: fffff8a000c45c58 Last contiguous PTE: fffffffffffffffc
Flags2: Inherit: 1
```

2.4.5   vadwalk

To inspect a process's VAD nodes in table form, use the vadwalk command.

```
$ vol.py -f win7.raw --profile=Win7SP0x64 vadwalk -p 296

Volatility Foundation Volatility Framework 2.6
***********************************************************************
Pid:   296
Address          Parent            Left              Right              Start              End                Tag
---------------- ----------------- ----------------- ----------------- ----------------- ----------------- ----
0xfffffa8000c00620 0x0000000000000000 0xfffffa8000deaa40 0xfffffa8000c043d0 0x000000007f0e0000
0x000000007ffdffff VadS
0xfffffa8000deaa40 0xfffffa8000c00620 0xfffffa8000bc4660 0xfffffa80011b8d80 0x0000000000ae0000
0x0000000000b1ffff VadS
0xfffffa8000bc4660 0xfffffa8000deaa40 0xfffffa8000c04260 0xfffffa8000c91010 0x00000000004d0000
0x0000000000650fff Vadm
0xfffffa8000c04260 0xfffffa8000bc4660 0xfffffa8000c82010 0xfffffa80012acce0 0x00000000002a0000
0x00000000039ffff VadS
0xfffffa8000c82010 0xfffffa8000c04260 0xfffffa8000cbce80 0xfffffa8000c00330 0x00000000001f0000
0x00000000001f0fff Vadm
0xfffffa8000cbce80 0xfffffa8000c82010 0xfffffa8000bc4790 0xfffffa8000d9bb80 0x0000000000180000
0x0000000000181fff Vad
0xfffffa8000bc4790 0xfffffa8000cbce80 0xfffffa8000c00380 0xfffffa8000e673a0 0x0000000000100000
0x0000000000166fff Vad
0xfffffa8000c00380 0xfffffa8000bc4790 0x0000000000000000 0x0000000000000000
0x0000000000000000 0x00000000000fffff VadS
...
```

2.4.6   vadtree

To display the VAD nodes in a visual tree form, use the vadtree command.

```
$ vol.py -f win7.raw --profile=Win7SP0x64 vadtree -p 296

Volatility Foundation Volatility Framework 2.6
***********************************************************************
Pid:   296
 0x000000007f0e0000 - 0x000000007ffdffff
  0x0000000000ae0000 - 0x0000000000b1ffff
   0x00000000004d0000 - 0x0000000000650fff
    0x00000000002a0000 - 0x00000000039ffff
     0x00000000001f0000 - 0x00000000001f0fff
      0x0000000000180000 - 0x0000000000181fff
       0x0000000000100000 - 0x0000000000166fff
        0x0000000000000000 - 0x00000000000fffff
        0x0000000000170000 - 0x0000000000170fff
       0x00000000001a0000 - 0x00000000001a1fff
      0x0000000000190000 - 0x0000000000190fff
      0x00000000001b0000 - 0x00000000001effff
     0x0000000000240000 - 0x000000000024ffff
...
```

If you want to view the balanced binary tree in Graphviz format, just add **--output=dot --output-file=graph.dot** to your command.
Then you can open graph.dot in any Graphviz-compatible viewer. This plugin also supports color coding the output based on the regions that contain stacks, heaps, mapped files, DLLs, etc.

A partial example is shown below using Omnigraffle:

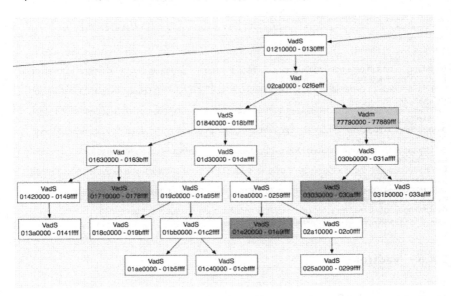

Fillcolor Legend:

- *Red: Heaps*
- *Gray: DLLs*
- *Green: Stacks*
- *Yellow: Mapped Files*

2.4.7   vaddump

To extract the range of pages described by a VAD node, use the vaddump command. This is similar to memdump, except the pages belonging to each VAD node are placed in separate files (named according to the starting and ending addresses) instead of one large conglomerate file. If any pages in the range are not memory resident, they're padded with 0's using the address space's zread() method.

```
$ vol.py -f win7.raw --profile=Win7SP0x64 vaddump -D vads

Volatility Foundation Volatility Framework 2.6
Pid      Process            Start         End          Result
-------- ------------------ ------------- ------------ ------
    4 System          0x0000000076d40000 0x0000000076eeafff
vads/System.17fef9e0.0x0000000076d40000-0x0000000076eeafff.dmp
    4 System          0x0000000000040000 0x0000000000040fff
vads/System.17fef9e0.0x0000000000040000-0x0000000000040fff.dmp
    4 System          0x0000000000010000 0x0000000000032fff
vads/System.17fef9e0.0x0000000000010000-0x0000000000032fff.dmp
    4 System          0x000000007ffe0000 0x000000007ffefff
vads/System.17fef9e0.0x000000007ffe0000-0x000000007ffefff.dmp
    4 System          0x0000000076f20000 0x000000007709ffff
vads/System.17fef9e0.0x0000000076f20000-0x000000007709ffff.dmp
  208 smss.exe        0x000000007efe0000 0x000000007ffdffff
vads/smss.exe.176e97f0.0x000000007efe0000-0x000000007ffdffff.dmp
  208 smss.exe        0x00000000003d0000 0x00000000004cffff
vads/smss.exe.176e97f0.0x00000000003d0000-0x00000000004cffff.dmp
  208 smss.exe        0x0000000000100000 0x0000000000100fff
vads/smss.exe.176e97f0.0x0000000000100000-0x0000000000100fff.dmp
  208 smss.exe        0x0000000000000000 0x00000000000fffff
vads/smss.exe.176e97f0.0x0000000000000000-0x00000000000fffff.dmp
  208 smss.exe        0x0000000000190000 0x000000000020ffff
vads/smss.exe.176e97f0.0x0000000000190000-0x000000000020ffff.dmp

$ ls -al vads/

total 123720
drwxr-xr-x 69 michaelligh  staff    2346 Apr  6 13:12 .
drwxr-xr-x 37 michaelligh  staff    1258 Apr  6 13:11 ..
-rw-r--r--  1 michaelligh  staff  143360 Apr  6 13:12 System.17fef9e0.0x0000000000010000-
0x0000000000032fff.dmp
-rw-r--r--  1 michaelligh  staff    4096 Apr  6 13:12 System.17fef9e0.0x0000000000040000-
0x0000000000040fff.dmp
-rw-r--r--  1 michaelligh  staff 1748992 Apr  6 13:12 System.17fef9e0.0x0000000076d40000-
0x0000000076eeafff.dmp
-rw-r--r--  1 michaelligh  staff 1572864 Apr  6 13:12 System.17fef9e0.0x0000000076f20000-
0x000000007709ffff.dmp
-rw-r--r--  1 michaelligh  staff   65536 Apr  6 13:12 System.17fef9e0.0x000000007ffe0000-
0x000000007ffefff.dmp
-rw-r--r--  1 michaelligh  staff 1048576 Apr  6 13:12 csrss.exe.176006c0.0x0000000000000000-
0x00000000000fffff.dmp
-rw-r--r--  1 michaelligh  staff  421888 Apr  6 13:12 csrss.exe.176006c0.0x0000000000100000-
0x0000000000166fff.dmp
-rw-r--r--  1 michaelligh  staff    4096 Apr  6 13:12 csrss.exe.176006c0.0x0000000000170000-
0x0000000000170fff.dmp
...
```

The files are named like this:

ProcessName.PhysicalOffset.StartingVPN.EndingVPN.dmp

The reason the PhysicalOffset field exists is so you can distinguish between two processes with the same name.

2.4.8   evtlogs

The evtlogs command extracts and parses binary event logs from memory. Binary event logs are found on Windows XP and 2003 machines, therefore this plugin only works on these architectures. These files are extracted from VAD of the services.exe process, parsed and dumped to a specified location.

```
$ vol.py -f WinXPSP1x64.vmem --profile=WinXPSP2x64 evtlogs -D output

Volatility Foundation Volatility Framework 2.6
Parsed data sent to appevent.txt
Parsed data sent to secevent.txt
Parsed data sent to sysevent.txt
```

There is also an option (--save-evt) to dump raw event logs for parsing with external tools:

```
$ vol.py -f WinXPSP1x64.vmem --profile=WinXPSP2x64 evtlogs
--save-evt -D output

Volatility Foundation Volatility Framework 2.6
Saved raw .evt file to appevent.evt
Parsed data sent to appevent.txt
Saved raw .evt file to secevent.evt
Parsed data sent to secevent.txt
Saved raw .evt file to sysevent.evt
Parsed data sent to sysevent.txt
```

Parsed output is pipe delimited to make it easier to import into excel files and the "messages" are separated by semicolons:

```
$ cat output/secevent.txt

2012-01-17 12:01:27|secevent.evt|MACHINENAME|S-1-5-18 (Local System)|Security|612|Success|-;-
;+;-;-;-;-;-;-;-;-;-;-;-;+;-;MACHINENAME$;;(0x0,0x3E7)
2012-01-17 17:06:18|secevent.evt|MACHINENAME|S-1-5-19 (NT Authority)|Security|528|Success|LOCAL
SERVICE;NT AUTHORITY;(0x0,0x3E5);5;Advapi;Negotiate;;-;MACHINENAME$(0x0,0x3E7);252;-;-;-
2012-01-17 17:06:18|secevent.evt|MACHINENAME|S-1-5-19 (NT Authority)|Security|576|Success|LOCAL
SERVICE;NT AUTHORITY;(0x0,0x3E5);SeAuditPrivilege        SeAssignPrimaryTokenPrivilege
SeImpersonatePrivilege
2012-01-17 17:06:19|secevent.evt|MACHINENAME|S-1-5-20 (NT
Authority)|Security|528|Success|NETWORK SERVICE;NT AUTHORITY;(0x0,0x3E4);5;Advapi;Negotiate;;-
;MACHINENAME$(0x0,0x3E7);252;-;-;-
2012-01-17 17:06:19|secevent.evt|MACHINENAME|S-1-5-20 (NT
Authority)|Security|576|Success|NETWORK SERVICE;NTAUTHORITY;(0x0,0x3E4);SeAuditPrivilege
SeAssignPrimaryTokenPrivilege        SeImpersonatePrivilege
```

If the --verbose flag is used, SIDs are also evaluated and placed in the parsed output instead of the defaulting raw SID. This action takes longer to run, since the plugin has to calculate each of the service SID and user SID from registry entries.

2.4.9 iehistory

This plugin recovers fragments of IE history index.dat cache files. It can find basic accessed links (via FTP or HTTP), redirected links (--REDR), and deleted entries (--LEAK). It applies to any process which loads and uses the wininet.dll library, not just Internet Explorer.

Typically that includes Windows Explorer and even malware samples.

```
$ vol.py -f exemplar17_1.vmem iehistory

Volatility Foundation Volatility Framework 2.6
**************************************************
Process: 1928 explorer.exe
Cache type "URL " at 0xf25100
Record length: 0x100
Location: Visited: foo@http://192.168.30.129/malware/40024.exe
Last modified: 2009-01-08 01:52:09
Last accessed: 2009-01-08 01:52:09
File Offset: 0x100, Data Offset: 0x0, Data Length: 0xa0
**************************************************
Process: 1928 explorer.exe
Cache type "URL " at 0xf25300
Record length: 0x180
Location: Visited:
foo@http://www.abcjmp.com/jump1/?affiliate=mu1&subid=88037&terms=eminem&sid=Z605044303%40
%40wMfNTNxkTM1EzX5QzNy81My8lM18FN4gTM2gzNzITM&a=zh5&mr=1&rc=0
Last modified: 2009-01-08 01:52:44
Last accessed: 2009-01-08 01:52:44
File Offset: 0x180, Data Offset: 0x0, Data Length: 0x108
**************************************************
...
```

2.5 NETWORKING

2.5.1 connections

To view TCP connections that were active at the time of the memory acquisition, use the connections command. This walks the singly-linked list of connection structures pointed to by a non-exported symbol in the tcpip.sys module.

This command is for **x86** and **x64 Windows XP** and **Windows 2003 Server** only.

```
$ vol.py -f Win2003SP2x64.vmem --profile=Win2003SP2x64 connections

Volatile Systems Volatility Framework 2.1_alpha
Offset(V)       Local Address           Remote Address          Pid
----------------- ----------------------- ----------------------- ------
0xfffffadfe6f2e2f0 172.16.237.150:1408    72.246.25.25:80         2136
0xfffffadfe72e8080 172.16.237.150:1369    64.4.11.30:80           2136
0xfffffadfe622d010 172.16.237.150:1403    74.125.229.188:80       2136
0xfffffadfe62e09e0 172.16.237.150:1352    64.4.11.20:80           2136
0xfffffadfe6f2e630 172.16.237.150:1389    209.191.122.70:80       2136
0xfffffadfe5e7a610 172.16.237.150:1419    74.125.229.187:80       2136
0xfffffadfe7321bc0 172.16.237.150:1418    74.125.229.188:80       2136
0xfffffadfe5ea3c90 172.16.237.150:1393    216.115.98.241:80       2136
0xfffffadfe72a3a80 172.16.237.150:1391    209.191.122.70:80       2136
0xfffffadfe5ed8560 172.16.237.150:1402    74.125.229.188:80       2136
```

Output includes the virtual offset of the _TCPT_OBJECT by default. The physical offset can be obtained with the -P switch.

2.5.2   connscan

To find _TCPT_OBJECT structures using pool tag scanning, use the connscan command. This can find artifacts from previous connections that have since been terminated, in addition to the active ones. In the output below, you'll notice some fields have been partially overwritten, but some of the information is still accurate.
For example, the very last entry's Pid field is 0, but all other fields are still intact. Thus, while it may find false positives sometimes, you also get the benefit of detecting as much information as possible.

This command is for x86 and x64 Windows XP and Windows 2003 Server only.

```
$ vol.py -f Win2K3SP0x64.vmem --profile=Win2003SP2x64 connscan

Volatility Foundation Volatility Framework 2.6
Offset(P)  Local Address           Remote Address          Pid
---------- ----------------------- ----------------------- ------
0x0ea7a610 172.16.237.150:1419     74.125.229.187:80       2136
0x0eaa3c90 172.16.237.150:1393     216.115.98.241:80       2136
0x0eaa4480 172.16.237.150:1398     216.115.98.241:80       2136
0x0ead8560 172.16.237.150:1402     74.125.229.188:80       2136
0x0ee2d010 172.16.237.150:1403     74.125.229.188:80       2136
0x0eee09e0 172.16.237.150:1352     64.4.11.20:80           2136
0x0f9f83c0 172.16.237.150:1425     98.139.240.23:80        2136
0x0f9fe010 172.16.237.150:1394     216.115.98.241:80       2136
0x0fb2e2f0 172.16.237.150:1408     72.246.25.25:80         2136
0x0fb2e630 172.16.237.150:1389     209.191.122.70:80       2136
0x0fb72730 172.16.237.150:1424     98.139.240.23:80        2136
0x0fea3a80 172.16.237.150:1391     209.191.122.70:80       2136
0x0fee8080 172.16.237.150:1369     64.4.11.30:80           2136
0x0ff21bc0 172.16.237.150:1418     74.125.229.188:80       2136
0x1019ec90 172.16.237.150:1397     216.115.98.241:80       2136
0x179099e0 172.16.237.150:1115     66.150.117.33:80        2856
0x2cdb1bf0 172.16.237.150:139      172.16.237.1:63369      4
0x339c2c00 172.16.237.150:1138     23.45.66.43:80          1332
0x39b10010 172.16.237.150:1148     172.16.237.138:139      0
```

2.5.3   sockets

To detect listening sockets for any protocol (TCP, UDP, RAW, etc), use the sockets command. This walks a singly-linked list of socket structures which is pointed to by a non-exported symbol in the tcpip.sys module.

This command is for x86 and x64 Windows XP and Windows 2003 Server only.

```
$ vol.py -f Win2K3SP0x64.vmem --profile=Win2003SP2x64 sockets

Volatility Foundation Volatility Framework 2.6
Offset(V)          PID  Port  Proto Protocol     Address          Create Time
------------------ ---- ----- ----- --------     ---------------- -----------
0xfffffadfe71bbda0  432 1025      6 TCP          0.0.0.0          2012-01-23 18:20:01
0xfffffadfe7350490  776 1028     17 UDP          0.0.0.0          2012-01-23 18:21:44
0xfffffadfe6281120  804  123     17 UDP          127.0.0.1        2012-06-25 12:40:55
0xfffffadfe7549010  432  500     17 UDP          0.0.0.0          2012-01-23 18:20:09
0xfffffadfe5ee8400    4    0     47 GRE          0.0.0.0          2012-02-24 18:09:07
0xfffffadfe606dc90    4  445      6 TCP          0.0.0.0          2012-01-23 18:19:38
0xfffffadfe6eef770    4  445     17 UDP          0.0.0.0          2012-01-23 18:19:38
0xfffffadfe7055210 2136 1321     17 UDP          127.0.0.1        2012-05-09 02:09:59
0xfffffadfe750c010    4  139      6 TCP          172.16.237.150   2012-06-25 12:40:55
0xfffffadfe745f610    4  138     17 UDP          172.16.237.150   2012-06-25 12:40:55
0xfffffadfe6096560    4  137     17 UDP          172.16.237.150   2012-06-25 12:40:55
0xfffffadfe7236da0  720  135      6 TCP          0.0.0.0          2012-01-23 18:19:51
0xfffffadfe755c5b0 2136 1419      6 TCP          0.0.0.0          2012-06-25 12:42:37
0xfffffadfe6f36510 2136 1418      6 TCP          0.0.0.0          2012-06-25 12:42:37
...
```

Output includes the virtual offset of the _ADDRESS_OBJECT by default. The physical offset can be obtained with the -P switch.

2.5.4   sockscan

To find _ADDRESS_OBJECT structures using pool tag scanning, use the sockscan command. As with connscan, this can pick up residual data and artifacts from previous sockets.

This command is for **x86** and **x64 Windows XP** and **Windows 2003 Server** only.

```
$ vol.py -f Win2K3SP0x64.vmem --profile=Win2003SP2x64 sockscan
```

Volatility Foundation Volatility Framework 2.6

Offset(P)	PID	Port	Proto	Protocol	Address	Create Time
0x0000000000608010	804	123	17	UDP	172.16.237.150	2012-05-08 22:17:44
0x000000000eae8400	4	0	47	GRE	0.0.0.0	2012-02-24 18:09:07
0x000000000eaf1240	2136	1403	6	TCP	0.0.0.0	2012-06-25 12:42:37
0x000000000ec6dc90	4	445	6	TCP	0.0.0.0	2012-01-23 18:19:38
0x000000000ec96560	4	137	17	UDP	172.16.237.150	2012-06-25 12:40:55
0x000000000ecf7d20	2136	1408	6	TCP	0.0.0.0	2012-06-25 12:42:37
0x000000000ed5a010	2136	1352	6	TCP	0.0.0.0	2012-06-25 12:42:18
0x000000000ed84ca0	804	123	17	UDP	172.16.237.150	2012-06-25 12:40:55
0x000000000ee2d380	2136	1393	6	TCP	0.0.0.0	2012-06-25 12:42:37
0x000000000ee81120	804	123	17	UDP	127.0.0.1	2012-06-25 12:40:55
0x000000000eeda8c0	776	1363	17	UDP	0.0.0.0	2012-06-25 12:42:20
0x000000000f0be1a0	2136	1402	6	TCP	0.0.0.0	2012-06-25 12:42:37
0x000000000f0d0890	4	1133	6	TCP	0.0.0.0	2012-02-24 18:09:07

...

2.5.5   netscan

To scan for network artifacts in **32 and 64-bit Windows Vista, Windows 2008 Server and Windows 7** memory dumps, use the netscan command. This finds TCP endpoints, TCP listeners, UDP endpoints, and UDP listeners. It distinguishes between IPv4 and IPv6, prints the local and remote IP (if applicable), the local and remote port (if applicable), the time when the socket was bound or when the connection was established, and the current state (for TCP connections only).

Please note the following:

- The netscan command uses pool tag scanning
- There are at least 2 alternate ways to enumerate connections and sockets on Vista+ operating systems. One of them is using partitions and dynamic hash tables, which is how the netstat.exe utility on Windows systems works. The other involves bitmaps and port pools.

```
$ vol.py -f win7.raw --profile=Win7SP0x64 netscan

Volatility Foundation Volatility Framework 2.6
Offset(P) Proto  Local Address        Foreign Address       State        Pid    Owner       Created
0xf882a30 TCPv4  0.0.0.0:135          0.0.0.0:0             LISTENING    628    svchost.exe
0xfc13770 TCPv4  0.0.0.0:49154        0.0.0.0:0             LISTENING    916    svchost.exe
0xfdda1e0 TCPv4  0.0.0.0:49154        0.0.0.0:0             LISTENING    916    svchost.exe
0xfdda1e0 TCPv6  :::49154             :::0                  LISTENING    916    svchost.exe
0x1121b7b0 TCPv4 0.0.0.0:135          0.0.0.0:0             LISTENING    628    svchost.exe
0x1121b7b0 TCPv6 :::135               :::0                  LISTENING    628    svchost.exe
0x11431360 TCPv4 0.0.0.0:49152        0.0.0.0:0             LISTENING    332    wininit.exe
0x11431360 TCPv6 :::49152             :::0                  LISTENING    332    wininit.exe
0x17de8980 TCPv6 :::49153             :::0                  LISTENING    444    lsass.exe
0x17f35240 TCPv4 0.0.0.0:49155        0.0.0.0:0             LISTENING    880    svchost.exe
0x17f362b0 TCPv4 0.0.0.0:49155        0.0.0.0:0             LISTENING    880    svchost.exe
0x17f362b0 TCPv6 :::49155             :::0                  LISTENING    880    svchost.exe
0xfd96570 TCPv4  -:0                  232.9.125.0:0         CLOSED       1      ?C?
0x17236010 TCPv4 -:49227              184.26.31.55:80       CLOSED       2820   iexplore.exe
0x1725d010 TCPv4 -:49359              93.184.220.20:80      CLOSED       2820   iexplore.exe
0x17270530 TCPv4 10.0.2.15:49363      173.194.35.38:80      ESTABLISHED  2820
iexplore.exe
0x17285010 TCPv4 -:49341              82.165.218.111:80     CLOSED       2820   iexplore.exe
0x17288a90 TCPv4 10.0.2.15:49254      74.125.31.157:80      CLOSE_WAIT   2820
iexplore.exe
0x1728f6b0 TCPv4 10.0.2.15:49171      204.245.34.130:80     ESTABLISHED  2820
iexplore.exe
0x17291ba0 TCPv4 10.0.2.15:49347      173.194.35.36:80      CLOSE_WAIT   2820
iexplore.exe
...
```

2.6 FILESYSTEM

2.6.1 mbrparser

Scans for and parses potential Master Boot Records (MBRs). There are different options for finding MBRs and filtering output.

While this plugin was written with Windows bootkits in mind, it can also be used with memory samples from other systems.

When run without any extra options, mbrparser scans for and returns information all potential MBRs defined by signature ('\x55\xaa') found in memory. Information includes: disassembly of bootcode (must have distorm3 installed) and partition information. This will most likely have false positives.

If distorm3 is not installed, the -H/--hex option can be used to get the entire bootcode section in hex instead of disassembly:

```
$ vol.py -f [sample] mbrparser -H
```

If the physical offset of the MBR is known, it can be specified with the -o/--offset= option for example:

```
$ vol.py -f [sample] -o 0x600 mbrparser
```

If the md5 hash of the desired bootcode is known, one can be specified using either the -M/--hash (the hash of bootcode up to the RET instruction) or -F/--fullhash (the hash of full bootcode) option.

```
$ vol.py mbrparser -f AnalysisXPSP3.vmem -M 6010862faee6d5e314aba791380d4f41
```

or

```
$ vol.py mbrparser -f AnalysisXPSP3.vmem -F 6010862faee6d5e314aba791380d4f41
```

In order to cut down on false positives there is a -C/--check option that checks the partition table for one bootable partition that has a known, nonempty type (NTFS, FAT*, etc).

```
$ vol.py -f [sample] -C mbrparser
```

There is also an option to change the offset for the start of the disassembly. This can be useful for investigating machines (like Windows XP) that only copy the part of the MBR bootcode that has not yet executed. For example, before changing the offset:

```
$ vol.py mbrparser -f AnalysisXPSP3.vmem -o 0x600

Volatility Foundation Volatility Framework 2.6
Potential MBR at physical offset: 0x600
Disk Signature: d8-8f-d8-8f
Bootcode md5: c1ca166a3417427890520bbb18911b1f
Bootcode (FULL) md5: c0bf3a94515bbd70e5a0af82f1804d89
Disassembly of Bootable Code:
0x00000600: 0000                 ADD [BX+SI], AL
0x00000602: 0000                 ADD [BX+SI], AL
0x00000604: 0000                 ADD [BX+SI], AL
0x00000606: 0000                 ADD [BX+SI], AL
0x00000608: 0000                 ADD [BX+SI], AL
0x0000060a: 0000                 ADD [BX+SI], AL
0x0000060c: 0000                 ADD [BX+SI], AL
0x0000060e: 0000                 ADD [BX+SI], AL
0x00000610: 0000                 ADD [BX+SI], AL
0x00000612: 0000                 ADD [BX+SI], AL
0x00000614: 0000                 ADD [BX+SI], AL
0x00000616: 0000                 ADD [BX+SI], AL
0x00000618: 0000                 ADD [BX+SI], AL
0x0000061a: 00bdbe07             ADD [DI+0x7be], BH
0x0000061e: b104                 MOV CL, 0x4
0x00000620: 386e00               CMP [BP+0x0], CH
...
```

After changing the starting offset:

```
$ vol.py mbrparser -f AnalysisXPSP3.vmem -o 0x600 -D 0x1b

Volatility Foundation Volatility Framework 2.6
Potential MBR at physical offset: 0x600
Disk Signature: d8-8f-d8-8f
Bootcode md5: 961f3ad835d6fa9396e60ea9f825c393
Bootcode (FULL) md5: f54546c199c72389f20d537997d50c66
Disassembly of Bootable Code:
0x0000061b: bdbe07              MOV BP, 0x7be
0x0000061e: b104                MOV CL, 0x4
0x00000620: 386e00               CMP [BP+0x0], CH
0x00000623: 7c09                JL 0x13
0x00000625: 7513                JNZ 0x1f
0x00000627: 83c510               ADD BP, 0x10
0x0000062a: e2f4                LOOP 0x5
...
```

2.6.2   mftparser

This plugin scans for potential Master File Table (MFT) entries in memory (using "FILE" and "BAAD" signatures) and prints out information for certain attributes, currently: $FILE_NAME ($FN), $STANDARD_INFORMATION ($SI), $FNan d $SI attributes from the $ATTRIBUTE_LIST, $OBJECT_ID (default output only) and resident $DATA. This plugin has room for expansion, however, and VTypes for other attributes are already included.

Options of interest include:

- --machine - Machine name to add to timeline header (useful when combining timelines from multiple machines)
- -D/--dump-dir - Output directory to which resident data files are dumped
- --output=body - print output in Sleuthkit 3.X body format
- --no-check - Prints out all entries including those with null timestamps
- -E/--entry-size - Changes the default 1024 byte MFT entry size.
- -O/--offset - Prints out the MFT entry at a give offset (comma delimited)

This plugin may take a while to run before seeing output, since it scans first and then builds the directory tree for full file paths.

Example (default output):

```
$ vol.py -f winxp.vmem mftparser

Volatility Foundation Volatility Framework 2.6
Scanning for MFT entries and building directory, this can take a while
[...]
************************************************************************
MFT entry found at offset 0x1e69c00
Type: File
Record Number: 12091
Link count: 2

$STANDARD_INFORMATION
Creation            Modified            MFT Altered         Access Date          Type
------------------- ------------------- ------------------- -------------------- ----
2010-02-27 20:12:32 2010-02-27 20:12:32 2010-02-27 20:12:32 2010-02-27 20:12:32 Archive

$FILE_NAME
Creation            Modified            MFT Altered         Access Date          Name/Path
------------------- ------------------- ------------------- -------------------- ---------
2010-02-27 20:12:32 2010-02-27 20:12:32 2010-02-27 20:12:32 2010-02-27 20:12:32 Documents
and Settings\Administrator\Cookies\ADMINI~1.TXT

$FILE_NAME
Creation            Modified            MFT Altered         Access Date          Name/Path
------------------- ------------------- ------------------- -------------------- ---------
2010-02-27 20:12:32 2010-02-27 20:12:32 2010-02-27 20:12:32 2010-02-27 20:12:32 Documents
and Settings\Administrator\Cookies\administrator@search-network-plus[1].txt

$DATA
0000000000: 65 78 70 0a 31 39 0a 73 65 61 72 63 68 2d 6e 65   exp.19.search-ne
0000000010: 74 77 6f 72 6b 2d 70 6c 75 73 2e 63 6f 6d 2f 0a   twork-plus.com/.
0000000020: 31 35 33 36 0a 33 03 00 32 34 33 33 39 32 30 0a   1536.3..2433920.
0000000030: 33 30 30 36 32 36 30 35 0a 38 33 37 34 31 36 35   30062605.8374165
0000000040: 37 36 0a 33 30 30 36 32 35 36 39 0a 2a 0a         76.30062569.*.

************************************************************************
[...]
************************************************************************
MFT entry found at offset 0x1cdbac00
Type: In Use & File
Record Number: 12079
Link count: 1

$STANDARD_INFORMATION
Creation            Modified            MFT Altered         Access Date          Type
------------------- ------------------- ------------------- -------------------- ----
2010-02-27 20:12:28 2010-02-27 20:12:28 2010-02-27 20:12:28 2010-02-27 20:12:28 Archive

$FILE_NAME
Creation            Modified            MFT Altered         Access Date          Name/Path
------------------- ------------------- ------------------- -------------------- ---------
2010-02-27 20:12:28 2010-02-27 20:12:28 2010-02-27 20:12:28 2010-02-27 20:12:28 Documents
and Settings\Administrator\Local Settings\Temp\plugtmp\PDF.php

$DATA
Non-Resident

************************************************************************
...
```

The bodyfile output is also an option. It is recommended that the output be stored in a file using the --output-file option, since it is quite lengthy. The following shows creating a bodyfile using **mftparser** while dumping resident files. You can also see a file of interest that is created on the system (f.txt) which happens to be recovered in the output directory:

```
$ vol.py -f grrcon.img mftparser --output=body -D output --output-file=grrcon_mft.body

Volatility Foundation Volatility Framework 2.6
Scanning for MFT entries and building directory, this can take a while

$ cat grrcon_mft.body

[...]
0|[MFT STD_INFO] WINDOWS\system32\systems (Offset: 0x15938400)|12029|---------------
|0|0|0|1335579320|1335579320|1335579320|1335578463
0|[MFT FILE_NAME] WINDOWS\system32\systems\f.txt (Offset: 0x15938800)|12030|---a-----------
|0|0|0|1335578503|1335578503|1335578503|1335578503
0|[MFT STD_INFO] WINDOWS\system32\systems\f.txt (Offset: 0x15938800)|12030|---a-----------
|0|0|0|1335578503|1335578503|1335578503|1335578503
0|[MFT FILE_NAME] WINDOWS\system32\systems\g.exe (Offset: 0x15938c00)|12031|---a-----------
|0|0|0|1335578514|1335578514|1335578514|1335578514
0|[MFT STD_INFO] WINDOWS\system32\systems\g.exe (Offset: 0x15938c00)|12031|---a-----------
|0|0|0|1335579014|1335578514|1335578514|1335578514
0|[MFT FILE_NAME] WINDOWS\inf\divasrv.inf (Offset: 0x15c83000)|2192|---a-----------
|0|0|22554|1332601266|1332601266|1332601266|1332601235
[...]

$ ls output/*15938800*

output/file.0x15938800.data0.dmp

$ cat output/*15938800*

open 66.32.119.38
jack
2awes0me
lcd c:\WINDOWS\System32\systems
cd /home/jack
binary
mput "*.txt"
disconnect
bye
```

The Sleuthkit **mactime** utility can then be used to output the bodyfile in a readable manner:

```
$ mactime -b grrcon_mft.body -d -z UTC | less

...
Sat Apr 28 2012 02:01:43,0,macb,---a----------,0,0,12030,"[MFT FILE_NAME]
WINDOWS\system32\systems\f.txt (Offset: 0x15938800)"
Sat Apr 28 2012 02:01:43,0,macb,---a----------,0,0,12030,"[MFT STD_INFO]
WINDOWS\system32\systems\f.txt (Offset: 0x15938800)"
Sat Apr 28 2012 02:01:54,0,macb,---a----------,0,0,12031,"[MFT FILE_NAME]
WINDOWS\system32\systems\g.exe (Offset: 0x15938c00)"
Sat Apr 28 2012 02:01:54,0,m.cb,---a----------,0,0,12031,"[MFT STD_INFO]
WINDOWS\system32\systems\g.exe (Offset: 0x15938c00)"
Sat Apr 28 2012 02:02:05,0,macb,---a----------,0,0,12032,"[MFT FILE_NAME]
WINDOWS\system32\systems\p.exe (Offset: 0x18229000)"
Sat Apr 28 2012 02:02:05,0,...b,---a----------,0,0,12032,"[MFT STD_INFO]
WINDOWS\system32\systems\p.exe (Offset: 0x18229000)"
Sat Apr 28 2012 02:02:06,0,m...,---a----------,0,0,12032,"[MFT STD_INFO]
WINDOWS\system32\systems\p.exe (Offset: 0x18229000)"
Sat Apr 28 2012 02:02:17,0,macb,---a----------,0,0,12033,"[MFT FILE_NAME]
WINDOWS\system32\systems\r.exe (Offset: 0x18229400)"
Sat Apr 28 2012 02:02:17,0,m.cb,---a----------,0,0,12033,"[MFT STD_INFO]
WINDOWS\system32\systems\r.exe (Offset: 0x18229400)"
Sat Apr 28 2012 02:02:26,0,macb,---a----------,0,0,12034,"[MFT FILE_NAME]
WINDOWS\system32\systems\sysmon.exe (Offset: 0x18229800)"
Sat Apr 28 2012 02:02:26,0,...b,---a----------,0,0,12034,"[MFT STD_INFO]
WINDOWS\system32\systems\sysmon.exe (Offset: 0x18229800)"
Sat Apr 28 2012 02:02:27,0,m.c.,---a----------,0,0,12034,"[MFT STD_INFO]
WINDOWS\system32\systems\sysmon.exe (Offset: 0x18229800)"
```

2.7 WINDOWS REGISTRY

Volatility has the ability to carve the Windows registry data.

2.7.1 Hivescan

To find the physical addresses of CMHIVEs (registry hives) in memory, use the hivescan command.

This plugin isn't generally useful by itself. It's meant to be inherited by other plugins (such as hivelist below) that build on and interpret the information found in CMHIVEs.

```
$ vol.py -f win7.raw --profile=Win7SP0x64 hivescan

Volatility Foundation Volatility Framework 2.6
Offset(P)
------------------
0x0000000008c95010
0x000000000aa1a010
0x000000000acf9010
0x000000000b1a9010
0x000000000c2b4010
0x000000000cd20010
0x000000000da51010
...
```

2.7.2   hivelist

To locate the virtual addresses of registry hives in memory, and the full paths to the corresponding hive on disk, use the hivelist command. If you want to print values from a certain hive, run this command first so you can see the address of the hives.

```
$ vol.py -f win7.raw --profile=Win7SP0x64 hivelist

Volatility Foundation Volatility Framework 2.6
Virtual        Physical          Name
----------------- ------------------ ----
0xfffff8a001053010 0x000000000b1a9010 \??\C:\System Volume Information\Syscache.hve
0xfffff8a0016a7420 0x0000000012329420 \REGISTRY\MACHINE\SAM
0xfffff8a0017462a0 0x00000000101822a0 \??\C:\Windows\ServiceProfiles\NetworkService\NTUSER.DAT
0xfffff8a001abe420 0x000000000eae0420 \??\C:\Windows\ServiceProfiles\LocalService\NTUSER.DAT
0xfffff8a002ccf010 0x0000000014659010
\??\C:\Users\testing\AppData\Local\Microsoft\Windows\UsrClass.dat
0xfffff80002b53b10 0x000000000a441b10 [no name]
0xfffff8a00000d010 0x000000000ddc6010 [no name]
0xfffff8a000022010 0x000000000da51010 \REGISTRY\MACHINE\SYSTEM
0xfffff8a00005c010 0x000000000dacd010 \REGISTRY\MACHINE\HARDWARE
0xfffff8a00021d010 0x000000000cd20010 \SystemRoot\System32\Config\SECURITY
0xfffff8a0009f1010 0x000000000aa1a010 \Device\HarddiskVolume1\Boot\BCD
0xfffff8a000a15010 0x000000000acf9010 \SystemRoot\System32\Config\SOFTWARE
0xfffff8a000ce5010 0x0000000008c95010 \SystemRoot\System32\Config\DEFAULT
0xfffff8a000f95010 0x000000000c2b4010 \??\C:\Users\testing\ntuser.dat
```

2.7.3   printkey

To display the subkeys, values, data, and data types contained within a specified registry key, use the printkey command. By default, printkey will search all hives and print the key information (if found) for the requested key. Therefore, if the key is located in more than one hive, the information for the key will be printed for each hive that contains it.

Say you want to traverse into the HKEY_LOCAL_MACHINE\Microsoft\Security Center\Svc key. You can do that in the following manner.

```
$ vol.py -f win7.raw --profile=Win7SP0x64 printkey -K "Microsoft\Security
Center\Svc"
Volatility Foundation Volatility Framework 2.6
Legend: (S) = Stable   (V) = Volatile

----------------------------
Registry: \SystemRoot\System32\Config\SOFTWARE
Key name: Svc (S)
Last updated: 2012-02-22 20:04:44

Subkeys:
  (V) Vol

Values:
REG_QWORD    VistaSp1     : (S) 128920218544262440
REG_DWORD    AntiSpywareOverride : (S) 0
REG_DWORD    ConfigMask   : (S) 4361
```

Here you can see how the output appears when multiple hives (DEFAULT and ntuser.dat) contain the same key "Software\Microsoft\Windows NT\CurrentVersion".

```
$ vol.py -f win7.raw --profile=Win7SP0x64 printkey -K
"Software\Microsoft\Windows NT\CurrentVersion"

Volatility Foundation Volatility Framework 2.6
Legend: (S) = Stable   (V) = Volatile

----------------------------
Registry: \SystemRoot\System32\Config\DEFAULT
Key name: CurrentVersion (S)
Last updated: 2009-07-14 04:53:31

Subkeys:
  (S) Devices
  (S) PrinterPorts

Values:
----------------------------
Registry: \??\C:\Users\testing\ntuser.dat
Key name: CurrentVersion (S)
Last updated: 2012-02-22 11:26:13

Subkeys:
  (S) Devices
  (S) EFS
  (S) MsiCorruptedFileRecovery
  (S) Network
  (S) PeerNet
  (S) PrinterPorts
  (S) Windows
  (S) Winlogon

...
```

If you want to limit your search to a specific hive, printkey also accepts a virtual address to the hive. For example, to see the contents of HKEY_LOCAL_MACHINE, use the command below. Note: the offset is taken from the previous hivelist output.

```
$ vol.py –f win7.raw --profile=Win7SP0x64 printkey -o 0xfffff8a000a15010

Volatility Foundation Volatility Framework 2.6
Legend: (S) = Stable   (V) = Volatile

----------------------------
Registry: User Specified
Key name: CMI-CreateHive{199DAFC2-6F16-4946-BF90-5A3FC3A60902} (S)
Last updated: 2009-07-14 07:13:38

Subkeys:
  (S) ATI Technologies
  (S) Classes
  (S) Clients
  (S) Intel
  (S) Microsoft
  (S) ODBC
  (S) Policies
  (S) RegisteredApplications
  (S) Sonic
  (S) Wow6432Node
```

2.7.4 hivedump

To recursively list all subkeys in a hive, use the hivedump command and pass it the virtual address to the desired hive.

```
$ vol.py -f win7.raw --profile=Win7SP0x64 hivedump -o 0xfffff8a000a15010

Volatility Foundation Volatility Framework 2.6
Last Written      Key
2009-07-14 07:13:38  \CMI-CreateHive{199DAFC2-6F16-4946-BF90-5A3FC3A60902}
2009-07-14 04:48:57  \CMI-CreateHive{199DAFC2-6F16-4946-BF90-5A3FC3A60902}\ATI Technologies
2009-07-14 04:48:57  \CMI-CreateHive{199DAFC2-6F16-4946-BF90-5A3FC3A60902}\ATI
Technologies\Install
2009-07-14 04:48:57  \CMI-CreateHive{199DAFC2-6F16-4946-BF90-5A3FC3A60902}\ATI
Technologies\Install\South Bridge
2009-07-14 04:48:57  \CMI-CreateHive{199DAFC2-6F16-4946-BF90-5A3FC3A60902}\ATI
Technologies\Install\South Bridge\ATI_AHCI_RAID
2009-07-14 07:13:39  \CMI-CreateHive{199DAFC2-6F16-4946-BF90-5A3FC3A60902}\Classes
2009-07-14 04:53:38  \CMI-CreateHive{199DAFC2-6F16-4946-BF90-5A3FC3A60902}\Classes\*
2009-07-14 04:53:38  \CMI-CreateHive{199DAFC2-6F16-4946-BF90-
5A3FC3A60902}\Classes\*\OpenWithList
2009-07-14 04:53:38  \CMI-CreateHive{199DAFC2-6F16-4946-BF90-
5A3FC3A60902}\Classes\*\OpenWithList\Excel.exe
2009-07-14 04:53:38  \CMI-CreateHive{199DAFC2-6F16-4946-BF90-
5A3FC3A60902}\Classes\*\OpenWithList\IExplore.exe
...
```

2.7.5   hashdump

To extract and decrypt cached domain credentials stored in the registry, use the hashdump command.

To use hashdump, pass the virtual address of the SYSTEM hive as -y and the virtual address of the SAM hive as -s, like this:

```
$ vol.py hashdump -f image.dd -y 0xe1035b60 -s 0xe165cb60

Administrator:500:08f3a52bdd35f179c81667e9d738c5d9:ed88cccbc08d1c18bcded317112555f4:::
Guest:501:aad3b435b51404eeaad3b435b51404ee:31d6cfe0d16ae931b73c59d7e0c089c0:::
HelpAssistant:1000:ddd4c9c883a8ecb2078f88d729ba2e67:e78d693bc40f92a534197dc1d3a6d34f:::
SUPPORT_388945a0:1002:aad3b435b51404eeaad3b435b51404ee:8bfd47482583168a0ae5ab020e1186a
9:::
phoenix:1003:07b8418e83fad948aad3b435b51404ee:53905140b80b6d8cbe1ab5953f7c1c51:::
ASPNET:1004:2b5f618079400df84f9346ce3e830467:aef73a8bb65a0f01d9470fadc55a411c:::
S----:1006:aad3b435b51404eeaad3b435b51404ee:31d6cfe0d16ae931b73c59d7e0c089c0:::
```

Hashes can now be cracked using John the Ripper, rainbow tables, etc.

It is possible that a registry key is not available in memory. When this happens, you may see the following error:

"ERROR : volatility.plugins.registry.lsadump: Unable to read hashes from registry"

You can try to see if the correct keys are available: "CurrentControlSet\Control\lsa" from SYSTEM and "SAM\Domains\Account" from SAM.

First you need to get the "CurrentControlSet", for this we can use volshell (replace [REGISTRY ADDRESS](SYSTEM) below with the offset you get from hivelist), for example:

```
$ vol.py -f XPSP3.vmem --profile=WinXPSP3x86 volshell

Volatility Foundation Volatility Framework 2.6
Current context: process System, pid=4, ppid=0 DTB=0x319000
Welcome to volshell Current memory image is:
file:///XPSP3.vmem
To get help, type 'hh()'
>>> import volatility.win32.hashdump as h
>>> import volatility.win32.hive as hive
>>> addr_space = utils.load_as(self._config)
>>> sysaddr = hive.HiveAddressSpace(addr_space, self._config, [SYSTEM REGISTRY ADDRESS])
>>> print h.find_control_set(sysaddr)
1
>>> ^D
```

Then you can use the printkey plugin to make sure the keys and their data are there. Since the "CurrentControlSet" is 1 in our previous example, we use "ControlSet001" in the first command:

```
$ vol.py -f XPSP3.vmem --profile=WinXPSP3x86 printkey -K "ControlSet001\Control\lsa"

$ vol.py -f XPSP3.vmem --profile=WinXPSP3x86 printkey -K "SAM\Domains\Account"

If the key is missing you should see an error message:

"The requested key could not be found in the hive(s) searched"
```

2.7.6   lsadump

To dump LSA secrets from the registry, use the lsadump command. This exposes information such as the default password (for systems with autologin enabled), the RDP public key, and credentials used by DPAPI.

```
$ vol.py -f laqma.vmem lsadump

Volatility Foundation Volatility Framework 2.6
L$RTMTIMEBOMB_1320153D-8DA3-4e8e-B27B-0D888223A588

0000   00 92 8D 60 01 FF C8 01                            ...`....

_SC_Dnscache

L$HYDRAENCKEY_28ada6da-d622-11d1-9cb9-00c04fb16e75

0000   52 53 41 32 48 00 00 00 00 02 00 00 3F 00 00 00   RSA2H.......?...
0010   01 00 01 00 37 CE 0C C0 EF EC 13 C8 A4 C5 BC B8   ....7...........
0020   AA F5 1A 7C 50 95 A4 E9 3B BA 41 C8 53 D7 CE C6   ...|P...;.A.S...
0030   CB A0 6A 46 7C 70 F3 21 17 1C FB 79 5C C1 83 68   ..jF|p....y...h
0040   91 E5 62 5E 2C AC 21 1E 79 07 A9 21 BB F0 74 E8   ..b^,..y....t.
0050   85 66 F4 C4 00 00 00 00 00 00 00 00 F9 D7 AD 5C   .f.............
0060   B4 7C FB F6 88 89 9D 2E 91 F2 60 07 10 42 CA 5A   .|........`..B.Z
0070   FC F0 D1 00 0F 86 29 B5 2E 1E 8C E0 00 00 00 00   ......)........
0080   AF 43 30 5F 0D 0E 55 04 57 F9 0D 70 4A C8 36 01   .C0_..U.W..pJ.6.
0090   C2 63 45 59 27 62 B5 77 59 84 B7 65 8E DB 8A E0   .cEY'b.wY..e....
00A0   00 00 00 00 89 19 5E D8 CB 0E 03 39 E2 52 04 37   ......^....9.R.7
00B0   20 DC 03 C8 47 B5 2A B3 9C 01 65 15 FF 0F FF 8F    ...G.*...e.....
00C0   17 9F C1 47 00 00 00 00 1B AC BF 62 4E 81 D6 2A   ...G.......bN..*
00D0   32 98 36 3A 11 88 2D 99 3A EA 59 DE 4D 45 2B 9E   2.6:..-.:.Y.ME+.
00E0   74 15 14 E1 F2 B5 B2 80 00 00 00 00 75 BD A0 36   t...........u..6
00F0   20 AD 29 0E 88 E0 FD 5B AD 67 CA 88 FC 85 B9 82    .)....[.g......
0100   94 15 33 1A F1 65 45 D1 CA F9 D8 4C 00 00 00 00   ..3..eE....L....
0110   71 F0 0B 11 F2 F1 AA C5 0C 22 44 06 E1 38 6C ED   q........"D..8l.
0120   6E 38 51 18 E8 44 5F AD C2 CE 0A 0A 1E 8C 68 4F   n8Q..D_.......hO
0130   4D 91 69 07 DE AA 1A EC E6 36 2A 9C 9C B6 49 1F   M.i......6*...I.
0140   B3 DD 89 18 52 7C F8 96 4F AF 05 29 DF 17 D8 48   ....R|..O..)...H
0150   00 00 00 00 00 00 00 00 00 00 00 00 00 00 00 00   ................
0160   00 00 00 00 00 00 00 00 00 00 00 00 00 00 00 00   ................
0170   00 00 00 00 00 00 00 00 00 00 00 00               ............
```

Possible items are:

- **$MACHINE.ACC**: Domain authentication Microsoft.
- **DefaultPassword**: Password used to log on to Windows when auto-login is enabled.
- **NL$KM**: Secret key used to encrypt cached domain passwords Decrypting LSA Secrets.
- **L$RTMTIMEBOMB_***: Timestamp giving the date when an unactivated copy of Windows will stop working.
- **L$HYDRAENCKEY_***: Private key used for Remote Desktop Protocol (RDP). If you also have a packet capture from a system that was attacked via RDP, you can extract the client's public key from the packet capture and the server's private key from memory; then decrypt the traffic.

2.7.7   userassist

To get the UserAssist keys from a sample you can use the userassist plugin.

```
$ vol.py -f win7.vmem --profile=Win7SP0x86 userassist

Volatility Foundation Volatility Framework 2.6
----------------------------
Registry: \??\C:\Users\admin\ntuser.dat
Key name: Count
Last updated: 2010-07-06 22:40:25

Subkeys:

Values:
REG_BINARY    Microsoft.Windows.GettingStarted :
Count:        14
Focus Count:  21
Time Focused:  0:07:00.500000
Last updated:   2010-03-09 19:49:20

0000   00 00 00 00 0E 00 00 00 15 00 00 00 A0 68 06 00    .............h..
0010   00 00 80 BF 00 00 80 BF 00 00 80 BF 00 00 80 BF    ................
0020   00 00 80 BF 00 00 80 BF 00 00 80 BF 00 00 80 BF    ................
0030   00 00 80 BF 00 00 80 BF FF FF FF FF EC FE 7B 9C    ..............{.
0040   C1 BF CA 01 00 00 00 00                            ........

REG_BINARY    UEME_CTLSESSION :
Count:        187
Focus Count:  1205
Time Focused:  6:25:06.216000
Last updated:   1970-01-01 00:00:00

[snip]

REG_BINARY    %windir%\system32\calc.exe :
Count:        12
Focus Count:  17
Time Focused:  0:05:40.500000
Last updated:   2010-03-09 19:49:20

0000   00 00 00 00 0C 00 00 00 11 00 00 00 20 30 05 00    ............ 0..
0010   00 00 80 BF 00 00 80 BF 00 00 80 BF 00 00 80 BF    ................
0020   00 00 80 BF 00 00 80 BF 00 00 80 BF 00 00 80 BF    ................
0030   00 00 80 BF 00 00 80 BF FF FF FF FF EC FE 7B 9C    ..............{.
0040   C1 BF CA 01 00 00 00 00                            ........
```

2.7.8   shellbags

Microsoft Windows uses a set of Registry keys known as "shellbags" to maintain the size, view, icon, and position of a folder when using Explorer.
Shellbags persist information for directories even after the directory is removed, which means that they can be used to enumerate past mounted volumes, deleted files, and user actions.

This plugin parses and prints Shellbag information obtained from the registry.

There are two options for output: verbose (default) and bodyfile format.

$ vol.py -f win7.vmem --profile=Win7SP1x86 shellbags

```
Volatility Foundation Volatility Framework 2.6
Scanning for registries....
Gathering shellbag items and building path tree...
*************************************************************************
Registry: \??\C:\Users\user\ntuser.dat
Key: Software\Microsoft\Windows\Shell\Bags\1\Desktop
Last updated: 2011-10-20 15:24:46
Value                   File Name     Modified Date         Create Date          Access Date           File Attr                Unicode Name
----------------------- ------------- --------------------- -------------------- --------------------- ------------------------ ------------
ItemPos1176x882x96(1)   ADOBER~1.LNK  2011-10-20 15:20:04   2011-10-20 15:20:04  2011-10-20 15:20:04   ARC
Adobe Reader X.lnk
ItemPos1176x882x96(1)   ENCASE~1.LNK  2011-05-15 23:02:26   2011-05-15 23:02:26  2011-05-15 23:02:26   ARC
EnCase v6.18.lnk
ItemPos1176x882x96(1)   VMWARE~1.LNK  2011-10-20 15:13:06   2011-05-15 23:09:08  2011-10-20 15:13:06   ARC
VMware Shared Folders.lnk
ItemPos1176x882x96(1)   EF_SET~1.EXE  2010-12-28 15:47:32   2011-05-15 23:01:10  2011-05-15 23:01:10   ARC, NI
ef_setup_618_english.exe
ItemPos1366x768x96(1)   ADOBER~1.LNK  2011-10-20 15:20:04   2011-10-20 15:20:04  2011-10-20 15:20:04   ARC
Adobe Reader X.lnk
ItemPos1366x768x96(1)   ENCASE~1.LNK  2011-05-15 23:02:26   2011-05-15 23:02:26  2011-05-15 23:02:26   ARC
EnCase v6.18.lnk
ItemPos1366x768x96(1)   EF_SET~1.EXE  2010-12-28 15:47:32   2011-05-15 23:01:10  2011-05-15 23:01:10   ARC, NI
ef_setup_618_english.exe
ItemPos1366x768x96(1)   VMWARE~1.LNK  2011-10-20 15:24:22   2011-05-15 23:09:08  2011-10-20 15:24:22   ARC
VMware Shared Folders.lnk
ItemPos1640x834x96(1)   EF_SET~1.EXE  2010-12-28 15:47:32   2011-05-15 23:01:10  2011-05-15 23:01:10   ARC, NI
ef_setup_618_english.exe
ItemPos1640x834x96(1)   ENCASE~1.LNK  2011-05-15 23:02:26   2011-05-15 23:02:26  2011-05-15 23:02:26   ARC
EnCase v6.18.lnk
ItemPos1640x834x96(1)   VMWARE~1.LNK  2011-05-15 23:09:08   2011-05-15 23:09:08  2011-05-15 23:09:08   ARC
VMware Shared Folders.lnk
*************************************************************************


*************************************************************************
Registry: \??\C:\Users\user\AppData\Local\Microsoft\Windows\UsrClass.dat
Key: Local Settings\Software\Microsoft\Windows\Shell\BagMRU
Last updated: 2011-10-20 15:14:21
Value  Mru  Entry Type   GUID                                  GUID Description    Folder IDs
------ ---- ------------ ------------------------------------- ------------------- ----------
1      2    Folder Entry 031e4825-7b94-4dc3-b131-e946b44c8dd5  Libraries           EXPLORER, LIBRARIES
0      1    Folder Entry 20d04fe0-3aea-1069-a2d8-08002b30309d  My Computer         EXPLORER, MY_COMPUTER
2      0    Folder Entry 59031a47-3f72-44a7-89c5-5595fe6b30ee  Users               EXPLORER, USERS
*************************************************************************


*************************************************************************
Registry: \??\C:\Users\user\AppData\Local\Microsoft\Windows\UsrClass.dat
Key: Local Settings\Software\Microsoft\Windows\Shell\BagMRU\0
Last updated: 2011-05-15 23:10:01
Value  Mru  Entry Type   Path
------ ---- ------------ ----
1      0    Volume Name  Z:\
0      1    Volume Name  C:\
*************************************************************************
...
```

Another option is to use the **--output=body** option for TSK 3.x bodyfile format. You can use this output option when you want to combine output from timeliner, mftparser and timeliner.

You can also include a machine identifier in the bodyfile header with the **--machine** flag (this is useful when combining timelines from multiple machines).
Only ITEMPOS and FILE_ENTRY items are output with the bodyfile format:

```
$ vol.py -f win7.vmem --profile=Win7SP1x86 shellbags --output=body

Volatility Foundation Volatility Framework 2.6
Scanning for registries....
Gathering shellbag items and building path tree...
0|[SHELLBAGS ITEMPOS] Name: Adobe Reader X.lnk/Attrs: ARC/FullPath: Adobe Reader X.lnk/Registry:
\??\C:\Users\user\ntuser.dat /Key: Software\Microsoft\Windows\Shell\Bags\1\Desktop/LW: 2011-10-20
15:24:46 UTC+0000|0|---------------|0|0|0|1319124004|1319124004|1319124004|1319124004
0|[SHELLBAGS ITEMPOS] Name: EnCase v6.18.lnk/Attrs: ARC/FullPath: EnCase v6.18.lnk/Registry:
\??\C:\Users\user\ntuser.dat /Key: Software\Microsoft\Windows\Shell\Bags\1\Desktop/LW: 2011-10-20
15:24:46 UTC+0000|0|---------------|0|0|0|1305500546|1305500546|1305500546|1305500546
0|[SHELLBAGS ITEMPOS] Name: VMware Shared Folders.lnk/Attrs: ARC/FullPath: VMware Shared
Folders.lnk/Registry: \??\C:\Users\user\ntuser.dat /Key:
Software\Microsoft\Windows\Shell\Bags\1\Desktop/LW: 2011-10-20 15:24:46 UTC+0000|0|---------------
|0|0|0|1319123586|1319123586|1305500948|1305500948
[snip]
0|[SHELLBAGS FILE_ENTRY] Name: Program Files/Attrs: RO, DIR/FullPath: C:\Program Files/Registry:
\??\C:\Users\user\AppData\Local\Microsoft\Windows\UsrClass.dat /Key: Local
Settings\Software\Microsoft\Windows\Shell\BagMRU\0\0/LW: 2011-05-15 23:03:35 UTC+0000|0|---------
------|0|0|0|1305500504|1305500504|1247539026|1247539026
0|[SHELLBAGS FILE_ENTRY] Name: Users/Attrs: RO, DIR/FullPath: C:\Users/Registry:
\??\C:\Users\user\AppData\Local\Microsoft\Windows\UsrClass.dat /Key: Local
Settings\Software\Microsoft\Windows\Shell\BagMRU\0\0/LW: 2011-05-15 23:03:35 UTC+0000|0|---------
------|0|0|0|1305500270|1305500270|1247539026|1247539026
...
```

2.7.9   shimcache

Shimcache, also known as AppCompatCache, is a component of the Application Compatibility Database, which was created by Microsoft (beginning in Windows XP) and used by the operating system to identify application compatibility issues.

This plugin parses the Application Compatibility Shim Cache registry key.

```
$ vol.py -f win7.vmem --profile=Win7SP1x86 shimcache

Volatility Foundation Volatility Framework 2.6
Last Modified            Path
---------------------------- ----
2009-07-14 01:14:22 UTC+0000  \??\C:\Windows\system32\LogonUI.exe
2009-07-14 01:14:18 UTC+0000  \??\C:\Windows\system32\DllHost.exe
2009-07-14 01:16:03 UTC+0000  \??\C:\Windows\System32\networkexplorer.dll
2009-07-14 01:14:31 UTC+0000  \??\C:\WINDOWS\SYSTEM32\RUNDLL32.EXE
2011-03-22 18:18:16 UTC+0000  \??\C:\Program Files\VMware\VMware Tools\TPAutoConnect.exe
2009-07-14 01:14:25 UTC+0000  \??\C:\Windows\System32\msdtc.exe
2009-07-14 01:15:22 UTC+0000  \??\C:\Windows\System32\gameux.dll
2011-08-12 00:00:18 UTC+0000  \??\C:\Program Files\Common Files\VMware\Drivers\vss\comreg.exe
2010-08-02 20:42:26 UTC+0000  \??\C:\Program Files\VMware\VMware Tools\TPAutoConnSvc.exe
2009-07-14 01:14:27 UTC+0000  \??\C:\Windows\system32\net1.exe
2009-07-14 01:14:27 UTC+0000  \??\C:\Windows\System32\net.exe
2011-08-12 00:06:50 UTC+0000  \??\C:\Program Files\VMware\VMware Tools\vmtoolsd.exe
2009-07-14 01:14:45 UTC+0000  \??\C:\Windows\system32\WFS.exe
...
```

2.7.10 getservicesids

The getservicesids command calculates the SIDs for services on a machine and outputs them in Python dictionary format for future use. The service names are taken from the registry ("SYSTEM\CurrentControlSet\Services").

```
$ vol.py -f WinXPSP1x64.vmem --profile=WinXPSP2x64 getservicesids

Volatility Foundation Volatility Framework 2.6
servicesids = {
 'S-1-5-80-2675092186-3691566608-1139246469-1504068187-1286574349':
'Abiosdsk',
 'S-1-5-80-850610371-2162948594-2204246734-1395993891-583065928': 'ACPIEC',
 'S-1-5-80-2838020983-819055183-730598559-323496739-448665943': 'adpu160m',
 'S-1-5-80-3218321610-3296847771-3570773115-868698368-3117473630': 'aec',
 'S-1-5-80-1344778701-2960353790-662938617-678076498-4183748354': 'aic78u2',
 'S-1-5-80-1076555770-1261388817-3553637611-899283093-3303637635': 'Alerter',
 'S-1-5-80-1587539839-2488332913-1287008632-3751426284-4220573165': 'AliIde',
 'S-1-5-80-4100430975-1934021090-490597466-3817433801-2954987127': 'AmdIde',
 'S-1-5-80-258649362-1997344556-1754272750-1450123204-3407402222': 'Atdisk',
...
```

In order to save output to a file, use the --output-file option.

2.7.11 dumpregistry

The dumpregistry plugin allows you to dump a registry hive to disk. It works on all supported Windows versions (Windows XP-8.1). By default the plugin will dump all registry files (including virtual registries like HARDWARE) found to disk, however you may specify the virtual offset for a specific hive in order to only dump one registry at a time. One caveat about using this plugin (or the dumpfiles plugin) is that there may be holes in the dumped registry file, so offline registry tools may crash if they are not made robustly to handle "corrupt" files. These holes are denoted in the text output with lines like Physical layer returned None for index 2000, filling with NULL. Example output is shown below:

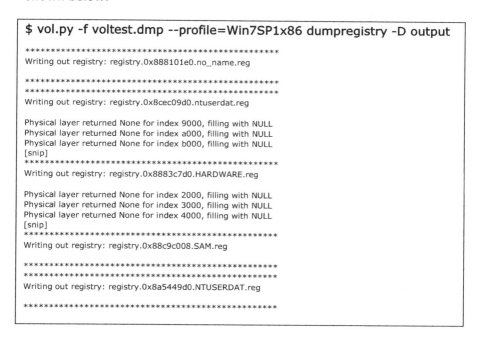

```
$ vol.py -f voltest.dmp --profile=Win7SP1x86 dumpregistry -D output
************************************************
Writing out registry: registry.0x888101e0.no_name.reg

************************************************
************************************************
Writing out registry: registry.0x8cec09d0.ntuserdat.reg

Physical layer returned None for index 9000, filling with NULL
Physical layer returned None for index a000, filling with NULL
Physical layer returned None for index b000, filling with NULL
[snip]
************************************************
Writing out registry: registry.0x8883c7d0.HARDWARE.reg

Physical layer returned None for index 2000, filling with NULL
Physical layer returned None for index 3000, filling with NULL
Physical layer returned None for index 4000, filling with NULL
[snip]
************************************************
Writing out registry: registry.0x88c9c008.SAM.reg

************************************************
************************************************
Writing out registry: registry.0x8a5449d0.NTUSERDAT.reg

************************************************
```

```
$ file output/*

output/registry.0x888101e0.no_name.reg:     MS Windows registry file, NT/2000 or above
output/registry.0x8881c008.SYSTEM.reg:       MS Windows registry file, NT/2000 or above
output/registry.0x8883c7d0.HARDWARE.reg:     data
output/registry.0x888c14e8.DEFAULT.reg:      MS Windows registry file, NT/2000 or above
output/registry.0x88c3b898.SECURITY.reg:     MS Windows registry file, NT/2000 or above
output/registry.0x88c9c008.SAM.reg:          MS Windows registry file, NT/2000 or above
output/registry.0x8a4c2008.NTUSERDAT.reg:    MS Windows registry file, NT/2000 or above
output/registry.0x8a5449d0.NTUSERDAT.reg:    MS Windows registry file, NT/2000 or above
output/registry.0x8c7e7008.BCD.reg:          MS Windows registry file, NT/2000 or above
output/registry.0x8cec09d0.ntuserdat.reg:    MS Windows registry file, NT/2000 or above
output/registry.0x8d432008.SOFTWARE.reg:     MS Windows registry file, NT/2000 or above
output/registry.0x945229d0.UsrClassdat.reg:  MS Windows registry file, NT/2000 or above
output/registry.0xa019c9d0.Syscachehve.reg:  MS Windows registry file, NT/2000 or above
```

Notice that the HARDWARE registry has "Data" as the type. This is because the first few cells of the registry are zeroed out. If you examine the registry with a hex editor, you will see valid keys and values:

```
$ xxd output/registry.0x8883c7d0.HARDWARE.reg |grep -v "0000 0000 0000 0000 0000
0000 0000 0000" | less

0001000: 6862 696e 0000 0000 0010 0000 0000 0000  hbin...........
0001020: a8ff ffff 6e6b 2c00 c1be 7203 3eba cf01  ....nk,...r.>...
0001030: 0000 0000 d002 0000 0300 0000 0100 0000  ...............
0001040: 9018 0000 2801 0080 0000 0000 ffff ffff  ....(..........
0001050: 7800 0000 ffff ffff 1600 0000 0000 0000  x..............
0001060: 0000 0000 0000 0000 0000 0000 0800 0000  ...............
0001070: 4841 5244 5741 5245 58ff ffff 736b 0000  HARDWAREX...sk..
0001080: 7800 0000 7800 0000 2800 0000 8c00 0000  x...x...(.......
0001090: 0100 0480 7000 0000 8000 0000 0000 0000  ....p...........
00010a0: 1400 0000 0200 5c00 0400 0000 0002 1400  ......\.........
00010b0: 3f00 0f00 0101 0000 0000 0005 1200 0000  ?...............
00010c0: 0002 1800 3f00 0f00 0102 0000 0000 0005  ....?...........
00010d0: 2000 0000 2002 0000 0002 1400 1900 0200   ... ...........
00010e0: 0101 0000 0000 0001 0000 0000 0002 1400  ...............
00010f0: 1900 0200 0101 0000 0000 0005 0c00 0000  ...............
0001100: 0102 0000 0000 0005 2000 0000 2002 0000  ........ ... ...
0001110: 0101 0000 0000 0005 1200 0000 0000 0000  ...............
0001120: a0ff ffff 6e6b 2000 3eb5 f30a 3eba cf01  ....nk .>...>...
0001130: 0000 0000 2000 0000 0500 0000 0100 0000  .... ..........
0001140: 6828 0200 701f 0080 0000 0000 ffff ffff  h(..p..........
0001150: 7800 0000 ffff ffff 1c00 0000 0000 0000  x..............
0001160: 0000 0000 0000 0000 0000 0000 0900 0000  ...............
0001170: 4445 5649 4345 4d41 5000 0000 0000 0000  DEVICEMAP......
0001180: f0ff ffff 6c66 0100 0802 0000 5379 7374  ....lf......Syst
0001190: a0ff ffff 6e6b 2000 00fc 6d03 3eba cf01  ....nk ...m.>...
00011a0: 0000 0000 2000 0000 0100 0000 0000 0000  .... ..........
00011b0: 8001 0000 ffff ffff 0000 0000 ffff ffff  ...............
00011c0: 7800 0000 ffff ffff 0c00 0000 0000 0000  x..............
00011d0: 0000 0000 0000 0000 0000 0000 0b00 0000  ...............
00011e0: 4445 5343 5249 5054 494f 4e00 0000 0000  DESCRIPTION.....
00011f0: f0ff ffff 6c66 0100 901b 0000 494e 5445  ....lf......INTE
0001200: f8ff ffff 181a 0000 a8ff ffff 6e6b 2000  ....nk .
0001210: b68f c70b 3eba cf01 0000 0000 9001 0000  ....>..........
0001220: 0300 0000 0200 0000 f012 0000 a05a 0080  .............Z..
0001230: 0800 0000 8017 0000 7800 0000 ffff ffff  ........x.......
0001240: 2c00 0000 0000 0000 2a00 0000 6600 0000  ,.......*...f...
0001250: 0000 0000 0600 0000 5379 7374 656d 0000  ........System..
0001260: d0ff ffff 766b 1500 1000 0000 9002 0000  ....vk.........
0001270: 0300 0000 0100 0000 436f 6d70 6f6e 656e  ........Componen
0001280: 7420 496e 666f 726d 6174 696f 6e00 0000  t Information...
...
```

THE LITTLE HANDBOOK OF WINDOWS MEMORY ANALYSIS

You may also dump only one registry at a time by using the virtual offset of the hive:

```
$ vol.py -f voltest.dmp --profile=Win7SP1x86 hivelist

Volatility Foundation Volatility Framework 2.6
Virtual    Physical   Name
---------- ---------- ----
[snip]
0x8cec09d0 0x0d1f19d0 \??\C:\Users\test\ntuser.dat
[snip]

$ python vol.py -f voltest.dmp --profile=Win7SP1x86 dumpregistry -o
0x8cec09d0 -D output/
Volatility Foundation Volatility Framework 2.6
****************************************************
Writing out registry: registry.0x8cec09d0.ntuserdat.reg

Physical layer returned None for index 9000, filling with NULL
Physical layer returned None for index a000, filling with NULL
Physical layer returned None for index b000, filling with NULL
Physical layer returned None for index c000, filling with NULL
Physical layer returned None for index d000, filling with NULL
Physical layer returned None for index e000, filling with NULL
Physical layer returned None for index f000, filling with NULL
Physical layer returned None for index 10000, filling with NULL
Physical layer returned None for index 11000, filling with NULL
Physical layer returned None for index 20000, filling with NULL
Physical layer returned None for index 21000, filling with NULL
```

```
$ file output/*

output/registry.0x8cec09d0.ntuserdat.reg: MS Windows registry file, NT/2000 or above
```

2.8 ANALYZE AND CONVERT CRASH DUMPS AND HIBERNATION FILES

Volatility supports memory dumps in several different formats, to ensure the highest compatibility with different acquisition tools.

You can analyze hibernation files, crash dumps, VirtualBox core dumps, etc in the same way as any raw memory dump and Volatility will detect the underlying file format and apply the appropriate address space.

You can also convert between file formats.

2.8.1   crashinfo

Information from the crashdump header can be printed using the crashinfo command. You will see information like that of the Microsoft dumpcheck utility.

```
$ vol.py -f win7_x64.dmp --profile=Win7SP0x64 crashinfo

Volatility Foundation Volatility Framework 2.6
_DMP_HEADER64:
Majorversion:        0x0000000f (15)
Minorversion:        0x00001db0 (7600)
KdSecondaryVersion   0x00000000
DirectoryTableBase   0x32a44000
PfnDataBase          0xfffff80002aa8220
PsLoadedModuleList   0xfffff80002a3de50
PsActiveProcessHead  0xfffff80002a1fb30
MachineImageType     0x00008664
NumberProcessors     0x00000002
BugCheckCode         0x00000000
KdDebuggerDataBlock  0xfffff800029e9070
ProductType          0x00000001
SuiteMask            0x00000110
WriterStatus         0x00000000
Comment              PAGEPAGEPAGEPAGEPAGEPAGE[snip]

Physical Memory Description:
Number of runs: 3
FileOffset    Start Address    Length
00002000      00001000         0009e000
000a0000      00100000         3fde0000
3fe80000      3ff00000         00100000
3ff7f000      3ffff000
```

2.8.2   hibinfo

The hibinfo command reveals additional information stored in the hibernation file, including the state of the Control Registers, such as CR0, etc. It also identifies the time at which the hibernation file was created, the state of the hibernation file, and the version of windows being hibernated. Example output for the function is shown below.

```
$ vol.py -f hiberfil.sys --profile=Win7SP1x64 hibinfo

IMAGE_HIBER_HEADER:
Signature: HIBR
SystemTime: 2011-12-23 16:34:27

Control registers flags
CR0: 80050031
CR0[PAGING]: 1
CR3: 00187000
CR4: 000006f8
CR4[PSE]: 1
CR4[PAE]: 1

Windows Version is 6.1 (7601)
```

2.8.3   imagecopy

The imagecopy command allows you to convert any existing type of address space (such as a crashdump, hibernation file, virtualbox core dump, vmware snapshot, or live firewire session) to a raw memory image. This conversion be necessary if some of your other forensic tools only support reading raw memory dumps.

The profile should be specified for this command, so if you don't know it already, use the kdbgscan or imageinfo commands first. The output file is specified with the -O flag. The progress is updated as the file is converted:

```
$ vol.py -f win7_x64.dmp --profile=Win7SP0x64 imagecopy -O copy.raw

Volatility Foundation Volatility Framework 2.6
Writing data (5.00 MB chunks): |......................................|
```

2.8.4   raw2dmp

To convert a raw memory dump (for example from a win32dd acquisition or a VMware .vmem file) into a Microsoft crash dump, use the raw2dmp command. This is useful if you want to load the memory in the WinDbg kernel debugger for analysis.

```
$ vol.py -f win7.raw --profile=Win7SP0x64 raw2dmp -O copy.dmp
Volatility Foundation Volatility Framework 2.6
Writing data (5.00 MB chunks): |...................................................................|
```

2.8.5   vboxinfo

To pull details from a virtualbox core dump, use the vboxinfo command.

```
$ vol.py -f win7sp1x64_vbox.elf --profile=Win7SP1X64 vboxinfo

Volatility Foundation Volatility Framework 2.6

Magic: 0xc01ac0de
Format: 0x10000
VirtualBox 4.1.23 (revision 80870)
CPUs: 1

File Offset        PhysMem Offset     Size
------------------ ------------------ ------------------
0x0000000000000758 0x0000000000000000 0x00000000e0000000
0x00000000e0000758 0x00000000e0000000 0x0000000003000000
0x00000000e3000758 0x00000000f0400000 0x0000000000400000
0x00000000e3400758 0x00000000f0800000 0x0000000000004000
0x00000000e3404758 0x00000000ffff0000 0x0000000000010000
0x00000000e3414758 0x0000000100000000 0x000000006a600000
```

2.8.6 vmwareinfo

Use this plugin to analyze header information from vmware saved state (vmss) or vmware snapshot (vmsn) files. The metadata contains CPU registers, the entire VMX configuration file, memory run information, and PNG screenshots of the guest VM.

```
$ vol.py -f Win7SP1x64-d8737a34.vmss vmwareinfo --verbose | less

Magic: 0xbad1bad1 (Version 1)
Group count: 0x5c

File Offset PhysMem Offset Size
---------- -------------- ----------
0x000010000 0x000000000000 0xc0000000
0x0c0010000 0x000100000000 0xc0000000

DataOffset   DataSize Name                                                Value
---------- ---------- -------------------------------------------------- -----
0x00001cd9      0x4 Checkpoint/fileversion                                0xa
0x00001cfc    0x100 Checkpoint/ProductName
0x00001cfc 56 4d 77 61 72 65 20 45 53 58 00 00 00 00 00 00   VMware.ESX......
0x00001d0c 00 00 00 00 00 00 00 00 00 00 00 00 00 00 00 00   ................
[snip]
0x00001e1d    0x100 Checkpoint/VersionNumber
0x00001e1d 34 2e 31 2e 30 00 00 00 00 00 00 00 00 00 00 00   4.1.0..........
0x00001e2d 00 00 00 00 00 00 00 00 00 00 00 00 00 00 00 00   ................
[snip]
0x00002046      0x4 Checkpoint/Platform                                   0x1
0x00002055      0x4 Checkpoint/usageMode                                  0x1
0x00002062      0x4 Checkpoint/memSize                                 0x1800
...
```

2.8.7   hpakinfo

This plugin shows info from an hpak formatted memory dump created by FDPro.exe.

```
$ vol.py -f memdump.hpak hpakinfo

Header:    HPAKSECTHPAK_SECTION_PHYSDUMP
Length:    0x20000000
Offset:    0x4f8
NextOffset: 0x200004f8
Name:      memdump.bin
Compressed: 0

Header:    HPAKSECTHPAK_SECTION_PAGEDUMP
Length:    0x30000000
Offset:    0x200009d0
NextOffset: 0x500009d0
Name:      dumpfile.sys
Compressed: 0
```

2.8.8   hpakextract

If you have an hpak file whose contents are compressed, you can extract and decompress the physical memory image using this plugin.

Andrea Fortuna

3. MEMORY ANALYSIS WORKFLOWS

3.1 MEMORY ACQUISITION ON PHYSICAL SYSTEM

One of the first steps that you need to perform when you deal with the forensic analysis of a compromised machine is to make a copy of volatile memory.

Here a shortlist of tools and techniques.

3.1.1 DUMPIT

DumpIt is a fusion of two trusted tools, **win32dd** and **win64dd**, combined into one one executable.
Simply double-click the DumpIt executable and allow the tool to run: the snapshot of the host's physical memory will be taken and saved into the folder where the executable was located.

This tool is a part of the Community edition of MoonSols Windows Memory Toolkit.

IMAGE CREATION PROCESS

1. Create a command prompt utilizing the local admin account of the target system and connect an external USB media to the device on which DumpIT will be in.

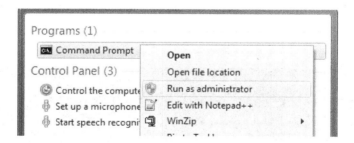

2. Navigate to the location where DumpIT is stored within the external HDD. Ensure that the external USB media has enough storage to store the memory.

3. Run DumpIT :

```
E:\>DumpIT.exe /Q /T RAW /N
```

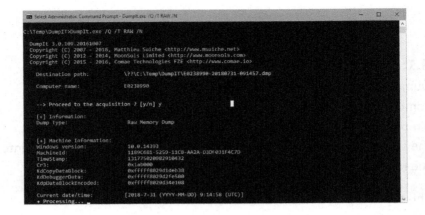

This will create a raw memory dump within the working directory that was used to start the dumpit executable. Successful execution will result in raw dump and a json file with metadata.

The files will utilize the following naming convention:

<hostname>-<YYYYMMDD>-<HHMMSS>.dmp

<hostname>-<YYYYMMDD>-<HHMMSS>.json

The screenshot below shows a successful creation of a memory dump.

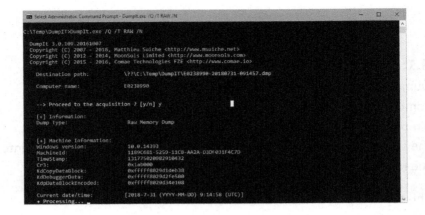

3.1.2 FTK Imager

Can acquire live memory and paging file on 32bit and 64bit systems.
Runs on **Windows 2003** and later versions

http://accessdata.com/support/adownloads#FTKImager

IMAGE CREATION PROCESS

1. Login to via local admin account on the target system.

2. Connect the external **HDD** into the target system.

5. Open Windows Explorer and navigate to the **FTK Imager Lite**
    folder within the external **HDD**.

6. Run **FTK Imager.exe** as an administrator (*right click -> Run as
    administrator*).

7. In FTK's main window, go to **File** and click on **Capture Memory**.

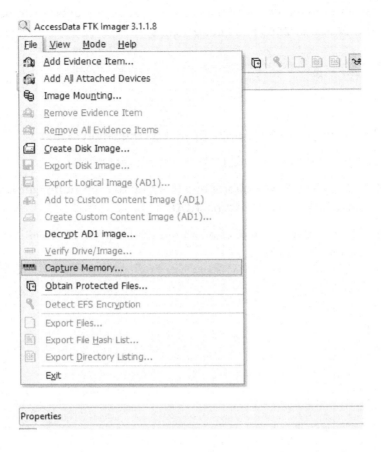

8. In the *Destination Path* browse for the correct collection folder, choose a filename according to naming policy and (optionally) select the *Include pagefile* checkbox. Finally click **OK**.

3.1.3 WINPMEM

Part of **Rekall Memory Analysis framework**, it supports **Windows XP** to **Windows 8**, both 32 and 64 bit architectures.

IMAGE CREATION PROCESS

Go to https://github.com/google/rekall/releases folder, download the correct version of WinPmem.exe and put it on the External HDD:

1. Select **winpmem-2.1.post4.exe** for windows system above Windows 2008
2. Select **winpmem_1.6.2.exe** for windows systems below Windows 2008

2. Create a command prompt utilizing the local admin account of the target system and connect an external USB/HDD to the device which WinPmem executable will be in.

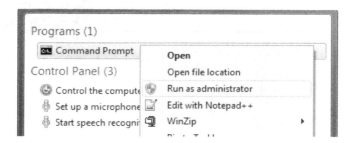

3. Navigate to the location where **WinPmem** is stored within the external HDD.
    Ensure that the external USB media has enough storage to store the memory dump.

4. Run **WinPmem** (please log the date, time and command used)

1. If using winpmem-2.1.post4.exe, follow the below command:

```
E:\> winpmem-2.1.post4.exe -o <destination path filename.aff4>
```

2. If using winpmem_1.6.2.exe, follow the below command:

```
E:\> winpmem_1.6.2.exe <destination path filename.aff4>
```

5. At the end of the collection, the **winpmem** driver will be unloaded automatically.

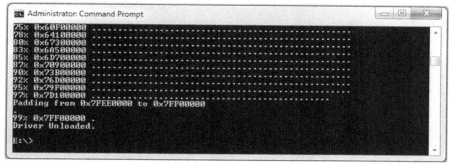

3.2 MEMORY ACQUISITION FROM A VIRTUAL MACHINE

3.2.1 VIRTUAL BOX

With the option **dumpvmcore --filename <name>** of VBoxManage, you can create a system dump of the running VM, which will be written into the given file.

This file will have the standard ELF core format (with some custom sections).

The dump format is described in the VirtualBox documentation:

The overall layout of the VM core format is as follows:

```
[ ELF 64 Header]
[ Program Header, type PT_NOTE ]
  → offset to COREDESCRIPTOR
[ Program Header, type PT_LOAD ] - one for each
contiguous physical memory range
  → Memory offset of range
  → File offset
[ Note Header, type NT_VBOXCORE ]
[ COREDESCRIPTOR ]
  → Magic
  → VM core file version
  → VBox version
  → Number of vCPUs etc.
[ Note Header, type NT_VBOXCPU ] - one for each
vCPU
[ vCPU 1 Note Header ]
  [ DBGFCORECPU - vCPU 1 dump ]
[ Additional Notes + Data ] - currently unused
[ Memory dump ]
```

(http://www.virtualbox.org/manual/ch12.html#ts_guest-core-format)

So, starting dump the memory into the ELF file:

```
$vboxmanage debugvm "Win7" dumpvmcore --filename test.elf
```

We're interested into the first LOAD section, that's where main memory reference is. We can get the correct offset using **objdump**:

```
$ objdump -h test.elf|egrep -w "(Idx|load1)"

Idx Name          Size      VMA               LMA                File off  Algn

 1 load1         40000000  0000000000000000  0000000000000000
00000720  2**0
```

So memory dump is in test.elf, starting at offset **0x720** and counting **0x40000000** bytes (1024Mb).

Now let's extract the RAM, getting rid of the first bytes:

```
$size=0x40000000;off=0x720;head -c $(($size+$off)) test.elf|tail -c
+$(($off+1)) > test.raw
```

Now the file **test.raw** contains a memory image that can be analyzed with Volatility:

```
$ volatility -f test.raw imageinfo

Volatility Foundation Volatility Framework 2.6

INFO : volatility.debug : Determining profile based on KDBG search...
Suggested Profile(s) : Win7SP1x86_23418, Win7SP0x86, Win7SP1x86
AS Layer1 : IA32PagedMemoryPae (Kernel AS)
AS Layer2 : FileAddressSpace (test.raw)
PAE type : PAE
DTB : 0x185000L
KDBG : 0x82944c30L
Number of Processors : 1
Image Type (Service Pack) : 1
KPCR for CPU 0 : 0x82945c00L
KUSER_SHARED_DATA : 0xffdf0000L
Image date and time : 2017-06-22 08:05:41 UTC+0000
Image local date and time : 2017-06-22 01:05:41 -0700
```

Obviously all commands can be wrapped in a simple bash script, in order to automate the extraction process:

```
#!/bin/bash
#Simple script for VirtuaBox memory extraction
# Usage: vboxmemdump.sh <VM name>

VBoxManage debugvm $1 dumpvmcore --filename=$1.elf

size=0x$(objdump -h $1.elf|egrep -w "(Idx|load1)" | tr -s " " |  cut -d
" " -f 4)

off=0x$(echo "obase=16;ibase=16;`objdump -h $1.elf|egrep -w
"(Idx|load1)" | tr -s " " |  cut -d " " -f 7 | tr /a-z/ /A-Z/`" | bc)

head -c $(($size+$off)) $1.elf|tail -c +$(($off+1)) > $1.raw

rm $1.elf
```

3.2.2 VMWARE

The process on a VMware machine is more simple than VirtualBox, just 4 simple steps:

- Suspend the virtual machine
- Navigate to the virtual machine's directory and identify the ***.vmem** file
- Copy the **vmem** image to you analysis workstation
- Finally use the following Volatility command to convert the memory image to a dump ready for analysis:

```
$ volatility -f memory_image.vmem -O raw_image --profile=Win7
raw2dump
```

3.3 MEMORY EXTRACTION FROM HIBERNATION FILES

The hibernation file (hiberfil.sys) is the file used by default by Microsoft Windows to save the machine's state as part of the hibernation process.

The operating system also keeps an open file handle to this file, so no user, including the Administrator, can read the file while the system is running, that needs to be extracted from a disk dump or using specific tools like **FTKImager**.

Although often presumed, the size of the hiberfil.sys is not one-to-one in size to the available, or total RAM of the machine.

Actually hibernation files consist of a standard header (**PO_MEMORY_IMAGE**), a set of kernel contexts and registers such as CR3 (**_KPROCESSOR_STATE**) and several arrays of compressed/encoded Xpress data blocks (**_IMAGE_XPRESS_HEADER** and **_PO_MEMORY_RANGE_ARRAY**).

The standard header exists at offset 0 of the file, the Signature member must be either "hibr" or "wake" to be considered valid, however in rare cases the entire **PO_MEMORY_IMAGE** header has been zeroed out, which can prevent analysis of the hibernation file in most tools.

In those cases, volatility will use a brute force algorithm to locate the data it needs.

The Xpress compression algorithm

Xpress algorithm has been implemented by Microsoft Exchange Team and is used for **LDAP** protocol, in Microsoft Embedded O.S. **Windows CE** and in **W**indows **IM**aging format (**WIM**).

According to Microsoft Exchange documentation, Xpress algorithm is:

- LZ77 + DIRECT2
- LZ77 for compression and DIRECT2 encode bytespositions in meta-data

Xpress has been publicly documented since Microsoft Interoperability initiative.

How to convert hiberfill.sys in a raw memory image for Volatility analysis?

Pretty simple, using the **imagecopy** Volatility plugin:

$ vol.py imagecopy -f hiberfil.sys -O hiber.img --profile=Win7SP1x64

```
$ vol.py -f hiberfil.sys -O hiber.img --profile=Win7SP1x64

Volatility Foundation Volatility Framework 2.6

Writing data (5.00 MB chunks):
|...............................................................................................
................................................................................................
................................................................................................
................................................................................................
......................................|
```

Now the hiber.img file can be analyzed with the usual methodology.

3.4 EXTRACT FORENSIC ARTIFACTS FROM PAGEFILE.SYS

Microsoft Windows uses a paging file, called **pagefile.sys**, to store page-size blocks of memory that do not current fit into physical memory.

This file, stored in *%SystemDrive%\pagefile.sys* is a hidden system file and it can never be read or accessed by a user, including **Administrator**.

It is possible to read this file by parsing the raw file system, or exact it using tools like **FTKImager**.

Contrary to **hybernation** files, page files cannot be processed with **Volatility**: in fact the page file is just the "holes" in memory where blocks are stored to disk, it will often contain information that can be relevant to the case you are trying to solve.

Because storage locations in the paging file are not necessarily sequential, it is unlikely to find consecutive pages there.
Although it is possible to find data in chunks smaller than or equal to **4KB**, its the largest an examiner can hope for.
So, the most productive method for analyzing paging files is searching for strings.

Analysis with "strings" command

To start your analysis on the page file you could use the **strings** command. Here some suggestions:

List all paths in pagefile:

```
$strings pagefile.sys | grep -i "^[a-z]:\\\\" | sort | uniq | less
```

Search for enviroment variables:

```
$ strings pagefile.sys | grep -i "^[a-zA-Z09_]*=.*" | sort -u | uniq | less
```

Search for URLs:

```
$ strings pagefile.sys | egrep "^https?://" | sort | uniq | less
```

Search for email addresses:

```
$ strings pagefile.sys | egrep '([[:alnum:]_.-]{1,64}+@[[:alnum:]_.-]{2,255}+?\.[[:alpha:].]{2,4})'
```

Analysis with YARA rules

Furthermore, you may scan the pagefile.sys using **YARA**.
Using (for example) the set of rules obtained with the method explained
in chapter 3.5, you may scan the pagefile in order to seek some
malware artifacts not found in the volatile memory:

```
$ yara malware_rules.yar pagefile.sys
```

3.5 FIND MALWARE IN MEMORY DUMPS

Using Yara rules and Volatility, is possible to a simple workflow useful for a first high-level analysis of memory dumps in order to search the presence of a generic malware.

The result of this workflow is useful as pivot-point for further analysis, focused on a specific threat.

The YARA rules repository

In the GitHub repository of **Yara Rules Project (https://github.com/Yara-Rules)**, a big set of precompiled rules is available, contains rules for a large number of threats, and a section specific for malwares.

During the first phase of a memory dump analysis, could be useful check the dump for the presence of artifacts related to the most known malware: but to performs this operation should be needed to scan the image with all rules located in "malware" section of repository.

In order to speed-up the process, i've developed a simple python script (*https://goo.gl/sZxar7*) for automatically download and merge rules from git repository:

```
andrea@Lucille:~/tmp/volsample$ ./malware_yara_rules.py

Cloning into 'rules'...
remote: Counting objects: 6166, done.
remote: Total 6166 (delta 0), reused 0 (delta 0), pack-reused 6166
Ricezione degli oggetti: 100% (6166/6166), 3.77 MiB | 2.15 MiB/s, done.
Risoluzione dei delta: 100% (3806/3806), done.
Processing ./rules/malware
Processing ./rules/malware/Operation_Blockbuster
Processing ./rules/malware/000_common_rules.yar
Processing ./rules/malware/APT_APT1.yar
Processing ./rules/malware/APT_APT10.yar
Processing ./rules/malware/APT_APT15.yar
Processing ./rules/malware/APT_APT17.yar
...
```

The output is a big **.yara** file containing all rules.

The memory analysis with Volatility
Although all Volatility commands can help you find malware, there are a few designed specifically for hunting rootkits and malicious code.

One of this is the "yarascan" plugin, that can help you locate any sequence of bytes (like assembly instructions with wild cards), regular expressions, ANSI strings, or Unicode strings in user mode or kernel memory.

Using the specific rules created in the previous step, you are able to hunt the presence of artifact related to most common malwares in the analyzed memory image.

So, first perform the image identification:

```
$ vol.py -f win7.raw imageinfo

Volatility Foundation Volatility Framework 2.6
Determining profile based on KDBG search...

Suggested Profile(s) : Win7SP0x64, Win7SP1x64, Win2008R2SP0x64, Win2008R2SP1x64
            AS Layer1 : AMD64PagedMemory (Kernel AS)
            AS Layer2 : FileAddressSpace (/Users/Michael/Desktop/win7.raw)
            PAE type : PAE
                 DTB : 0x187000L
                KDBG : 0xf80002803070
    Number of Processors : 1
    Image Type (Service Pack) : 0
        KPCR for CPU 0 : 0xfffff80002804d00L
        KUSER_SHARED_DATA : 0xfffff78000000000L
        Image date and time : 2012-02-22 11:29:02 UTC+0000
        Image local date and time : 2012-02-22 03:29:02 -0800
```

and then, simply perform the yara scan using the generated rules:

```
$ vol.py -f win7.raw --profile=Win7SP0x64 yarascan -y
malware_rules.yar

Volatility Foundation Volatility Framework 2.6


Rule: StuxNet_Malware_1
Owner: Process lsass.exe Pid 868

0x01002723 8b 45 08 35 dd 79 19 ae 33 c9 8b 55 08 89 02 89 .E.5.y..3..U....
0x01002733 4a 04 8b 45 08 c7 40 0c 77 35 00 01 33 c0 5e c9 J..E..@.w5..3.^.
0x01002743 c3 55 8b ec 83 ec 2c 83 65 e8 00 83 65 f4 00 83 .U....,.e...e...
0x01002753 65 e4 00 8b 45 20 8b 4d 14 8d 84 01 98 00 00 00 e...E..M........
0x01002763 89 45 f0 8d 45 f4 50 8d 45 e8 50 8d 45 d8 50 ff .E..E.P.E.P.E.P.
0x01002773 75 f0 ff 75 08 e8 14 fe ff ff 83 c4 14 89 45 fc u..u..........E.
0x01002783 83 7d fc 00 74 08 8b 45 fc e9 fd 00 00 00 8b 45 .}..t..E.......E
0x01002793 e8 89 45 f8 8b 45 e8 05 98 00 00 00 89 45 e8 c7 ..E..E.......E..
0x010027a3 45 e4 98 00 00 00 ff 75 20 ff 75 1c 8b 45 f8 05 E......u..u..E..
0x010027b3 84 00 00 00 50 8d 45 e4 50 ff 75 f4 8d 45 e8 50 ....P.E.P.u..E.P
0x010027c3 e8 79 fe ff ff 83 c4 18 8b 45 e8 89 45 dc ff 75 .y.......E..E..u
0x010027d3 14 ff 75 10 8b 45 f8 05 8c 00 00 00 50 8d 45 e4 ..u..E......P.E.
0x010027e3 50 ff 75 f4 8d 45 e8 50 e8 51 fe ff ff 83 c4 18 P.u..E.P.Q......
0x010027f3 8b 45 dc 89 45 ec 81 7d 14 00 10 00 00 72 47 8b .E..E..}.....rG.
0x01002803 45 ec 0f b7 00 3d 4d 5a 00 00 75 3a 8b 45 ec 8b E....=MZ..u:.E..
0x01002813 40 3c 05 f8 00 00 00 3b 45 14 73 2a 8b 45 ec 8b @<.....;E.s*.E..

Rule: StuxNet_Malware_1
Owner: Process lsass.exe Pid 868

0x01002eb5 74 36 8b 7f 08 83 ff 00 74 2e 0f b7 1f 8b 7f 04 t6......t.......
0x01002ec5 8d 5c 1f 02 8d 5b fe 3b df 7e 1d 66 83 7b fe 5c .\...[.;.~.f.{.\
0x01002ed5 75 f2 52 53 8d 5a 10 53 e8 bf ff ff ff ff 52 08 u.RS.Z......R.
...
```

The result of the scan highlights the presence of a stuxnet infection...now you can start a more specific analysis on target PIDs.

How to automate the whole process?

```
Image stuxnet.vmem identified as winXPSP2x86
*** Starting malware artifacts search...Yarascan...Malfind...Network...Done!
*** suspicious processes ***
        xtremeRATStrings: explorer.exe (1196)
                Saving process memory and handles...done!
                Scanning artifact with clamScan...OK
        StuxNet_Malware_1: lsass.exe (868)
                Saving process memory and handles...done!
                Scanning artifact with clamScan...win.Trojan.Duqu-10 FOUND
        StuxNet_Malware_1: lsass.exe (1928)
                Saving process memory and handles...done!
                Scanning artifact with clamScan...win.Trojan.Duqu-10 FOUND
        malfind: csrss.exe (600)
                Saving process memory and handles...done!
                Scanning artifact with clamScan...OK
        malfind: services.exe (668)
                Saving process memory and handles...done!
```

In order to help me in the day-by-day forensic practice, I've developed a small python script for automate the whole process of image identification, YARA rules parsing and report generation.

The project, named "Malhunt" is in continuous development, and all sourcecode is available on this github repository: https://github.com/andreafortuna/malhunt

The tool workflow is composed by 2 main steps:

1. **Identify suspicios processes**
   First, a list of suspicious preocesses is needed for further analysis.

   Malhunt uses the mixed result of 3 volatility plugin:

   i) **yarascan**: search suspicious processes trying to identify malware artifacts using a list of yara rules. This step is already explained in this article.
   ii) **malfind**: scans process memory in order to find some condition that may suggest some code injection (usually a memory area marked as Page_Execute_ReadWrite, which allows a piece of code to run and write itself).
   iii) **network scan**: using correct plugin according to Windows version (netscan or connscan), i extract a list of foreign

address and PIDs. If an ip is present into a blacklist (currently http://getipintel.net/), the related PID is added into the "suspiscios list".

2. Check processes for malware

In this second step Malhunt dumps all suspicious processes and related handles and check them with clamscan, in order to confirm the detection performed in the first step or mark it as false-positive.

If this workflow return even a single result, you have a good pivot point for further investigations.

3.6 TIMELINE CREATION

Required tools
Sleutkit (https://www.sleuthkit.org/sleuthkit/)

SleuthKit is a collection of command line tools that allows you to analyze disk images.

Volatility (http://www.volatilityfoundation.org/)

The well-known open source memory forensics framework for incident response and malware analysis.

The process

The traditional timeline analysis is generated using data extracted from the filesystem, enriched with information gathered by volatile memory analysis.
The data are parsed and sorted in order to be analyzed: the end goal is to generate a snapshot of the activity done in the system including its date, the artifact involved, action and source.

Here the steps, starting from a **E01** dump and a volatile memory dump:

1. Extract filesystem bodyfile from the .E01 file (physical disk dump):

```
fls -r -m / Evidence1.E01 > Evidence1-bodyfile
```

2. Run the **timeliner** plugin against volatile memory dump using volatility, after image identification:

```
vol.py -f Evidence1-memoryraw.001 --profile=Win7SP1x86 timeliner --output=body > Evidence1-timeliner.body
```

3. Run the **mftparser** volatility plugin, in order to spot some strange MFT activities.
   This step can generate duplicates entries against the fls output, but i think that this data can contain precious artifatcs.

```
vol.py -f Evidence1-memoryraw.001 --profile=Win7SP1x86 mftparser --
output=body > Evidence1-mftparser.body
```

4. Combine the **timeliner** and **mftparser** output files with the filesystem bodyfile

```
cat Evidence1-timeliner.body >> Evidence1-bodyfile
cat Evidence1-mftparser.body >> Evidence1-bodyfile
```

5. Extract the combined filesystem and memory timeline

```
mactime -d -b Evidence1-bodyfile 2012-04-02..2012-04-07 > Evidence1-
mactime-timeline.csv
```

6. Optionally, filter data using grep and applying the whitelist

```
grep -v -i -f Evidence1-mactime-timeline.csv > Evidence1-mactime-timeline-
final.csv
```

How to automate the whole process?

Similarly to Malhunt for malware search, I've also developed an automated tool for timeline creation: a brief python script, dubbed "Autotimeliner"(https://github.com/andreafortuna/autotimeliner).

The workflow used by **Autotimeliner** is similar to this above, with just a little addition (the **shellbags** timeline):

1. Identify correct volatility profile for the memory image.
2. Runs the **timeliner** plugin against volatile memory dump using volatility
3. Runs the **mftparser** volatility plugin, in order to extract $MFT from memory and generate a bodyfile
4. Runs the **shellbags** volatility plugin in order to generate a bodyfile of the user activity.
5. Merges the **timeliner, mftparser** and **shellbags** output files into a single **bodyfile**
6. Sorts and filters the **bodyfile** using **mactime** and exports data as **CSV**.

"Shellbags" are registry artifacts, used by Windows to store user preferences for GUI folder display within Windows Explorer, and may be used by a forensic analyst in order to reconstruct user activities.

Andrea Fortuna

ABOUT THE AUTHOR

Andrea started his career as programmer, then he moved to other experiences such as the help desk, system administration, IT Architecture and now he deal with cybersecurity in a multinational company.
In the spare time he likes to run, watching movies, playing and teaching music (he has a bachelor degree in guitar, but he love play and teach ukulele).

Made in the USA
Middletown, DE
22 April 2019